Restoring
Faith

Restoring Faith

America's
Religious Leaders
Answer Terror with Hope

Edited and with an Introduction by

Forrest Church

WALKER & COMPANY
New York

First published in the United States of America in 2001 by Walker Publishing Company, Inc.

Published simultaneously in Canada by Fitzhenry and Whiteside, Markham, Ontario L3R 4T8

The copyright in each sermon or address is held by its author, who has donated it for use in this book.

For information about permission to reproduce selections from this book, write to Permissions, Walker & Company, 435 Hudson Street, New York, New York 10014

John Gunnemann's sermon was previously published in the September 26–October 3 issue of *Christian Century*. © Christian Century Foundation 2001. Used by permission.

Library of Congress Cataloging-in-Publication Data available upon request
ISBN 0-8027-7632-9

BOOK DESIGN BY DEDE CUMMINGS/DCDESIGN

Printed in the United States of America

10 9 8 7 6 5 4 3 2 1

The events of this week are so unspeakable that it would be unfair for one pastor alone to have to give word to them. The tragedy of this week is so unthinkable that it would not be right for only one stream of thought to be given to it. The atrocities of this week were so unbelievable that it would not be reasonable for only one theological expression to be explored. The devastating events of this week are so monumental that not one of us, clergy or congregation, can stand alone and attempt to take them all in and still go on. We need one another. We cannot face it on our own. We must stand together, and so today we as your pastors and we as a congregation do. May we as a nation and a world do the same.

—Doretta M. Clark,
pastor, Mystic Congregational Church,
Mystic, Connecticut,
from a sermon on
September 16, 2001

Contents

꽃⭑꙰

Restoring
Faith

Introduction

I looked on the earth, and lo, it was waste and void,
And to the heavens, and they had no light.
I looked on the mountains, and lo, they were quaking,
And all the hills moved to and fro.
I looked, and lo, there was no one,
And all the birds of the air had fled.
I looked, and lo, the fruitful land was a desert,
And all its cities were laid in ruin. (Jer. 4:23-26)

JEW, CHRISTIAN, AND MUSLIM alike hold these words from the prophet Jeremiah sacred. How well they capture the sense of grief and horror that people across America felt immediately following the terrorist attack. Over the next seven days, faith communities throughout the nation gathered to mourn the innocent and to seek guidance from their religious leaders. It soon became evident that an act of terror designed to tear America apart had instead brought people together. Nowhere was this more manifest than in houses of worship. In unprecedented number, people thronged to churches, synagogues, and mosques to grieve together and comfort one another. To her Portland, Oregon, congregation, the Reverend Marilyn Sewell observed, "It is to these sacred spaces that we come to mourn collectively, that we come together in a community of love and faith that holds us when we falter, that reassures us that we are not alone, and that helps us to heal so that we may once again live lives of courage and hope."

The first work at hand was the work of mourning. In most worship services conducted during the week following Tuesday's tragedy, grief took precedence over anger. Tears were the sacrament of the hour. As the numbness of shock wore off, anxiety was left in its stead. Here the preachers pastored. How bracing and eloquent are the words of comfort these sermons offer.

Yet tears mingled with rage, fear, and doubt. Regardless of creed, the same questions echoed from the pews. How, as people of faith, must we respond? Where can we find God amid the rubble? Can we wage a holy war against Holy War? Is there hope for peace or are the trumpets of Armageddon less distant than before? These were the questions ministers, priests, imams, and rabbis had to address from their pulpits. Even as they spoke, the soul map of our nation was being recharted. The preachers' daunting task was to bring hope and direction to a people newly lost.

I have not heard of a single religious leader who didn't scrap his or her planned sermon in answer to the emergency 911 call. Not since the weekend following

President John F. Kennedy's assassination has any single event so focused religious proclamation in our country. The Reverend J. Philip Wogaman of Foundry United Methodist Church (right down the street from the White House), had devoted his Tuesday to traveling the Washington Metro subway system in preparation for his intended sermon on the people of Washington. At 9:05 A.M., his train stopped at the Pentagon. "A handful of people got off, nothing worth mentioning, although I planned to note in my sermon that this was the nerve center of the mightiest military force in the world." Minutes later the Pentagon was hit. Along with every other preacher in the nation, Wogaman began preparing a much more difficult sermon.

In a sense, the entire country became a house of worship. Bishop Hays Rockwell of the Episcopal Diocese of Missouri, underscored this in a letter he wrote the following Tuesday. "Driving the roads through the small communities southwest of St. Louis, you see the primitive plastic signs outside filling stations and run-down little shops. Most of the time those signs say things like 'bait,' 'ammo,' 'hot coffee.' Over the weekend after the catastrophe they said, 'God Bless America.'" Father William J. Bausche of St. Denis Roman Catholic Church in Manasquan, New Jersey, noted, "Even the TV stations which put out the most salacious fare . . . are saying, 'We are suspending our programs in the light of these events. Our thoughts and prayers are with the victims." The Reverend Brian Jordan, a Franciscan priest, gave the Eucharist to a construction worker laboring at Ground Zero who wanted to receive it in "God's House." The priest followed him to the shell of Six World Trade Center, where two iron beams welded in the shape of a cross stood out amid the wreckage. "There are no atheists at Ground Zero," Jordan said. "Everyone has a spiritual life now."

The memorials that began on Tuesday, continuing on Friday in the National Cathedral, and then conducted in houses of worship all around the country the following weekend, were not (as funerals often are) services of closure. They were invocations of a long and challenging journey that the American people will be taking together for years to come. In England's darkest hour, Winston Churchill said. "This is not the end. It is not even the beginning of the end. But it is, perhaps, the end of the beginning." Half a century later, many preachers sounded the same refrain: These acts of terror have transfigured our lives, initially and poignantly for the worse, but, potentially, also for the better. Witnesses to so many acts of sacrifice, valor, and kindness, few of us would wish to return to being the same individuals we were before September 11. More cognizant today of what really matters, we have become, at least for the moment, different people. In the days following the attack, in New York City, people asked strangers in elevators if they were okay. All across the land neighbors became family. And few of us failed to see our loved ones with new eyes.

In my counseling, I talked to people who finally, after months, even years of procrastination or rationalization, were ready to commit themselves to make something finer of their lives. "I've finally stopped drinking for good," one man told me. "I haven't been to church for twenty years," another confessed, "I've got to get my spiritual life in order." A third almost wept, "This has brought my husband and me back together. It's a miracle. I can't believe it. We've lost three friends. A dear cousin. And yet somehow in the midst of this tragedy we found one another." The shadow of death brought them back to life again.

The hope expressed in these sermons is not untempered by harsh realities. The world has changed. We face great and continuing dangers. It will be hard to fight a just war against terrorism, mindful of the need for proportionality, and it will be hard to win such a war even if we do strike the right balance. Thousands of innocent lives have been taken. Tens of thousands more have been ripped apart. The rest of us will struggle with new fears and anxieties. Our economic future is uncertain. The fabric of our society has been torn and will require years of mending. But, if our nation's religious leaders' confidence is not misplaced, this almost unimaginable tragedy will work its way deep into our very being and turn the lock of our souls.

The sermons excerpted in this wide-ranging collection were preached on Wednesday evening at candlelit memorial services, on Friday in mosques, Sunday in churches, and Monday and Tuesday to mark Rosh HaShanah and the beginning of the Jewish Days of Awe. Many of the preachers themselves were profoundly wounded: the Catholic priest who lost his brother; the minister who mourned five dead parishioners; the minister who turned to therapy and finally cried; the minister and airline pilot who was haunted by his knowledge of what his fellow pilots' final moments must have been like. And yet each of these beautiful sermons is, in one way or another, a testament of hope. If these preachers are right, by meeting the challenge that terrorism presents to our national will and capacity, and by rising to the spiritual challenge these terrible events present, our individual lives will be enriched, relationships will deepen, and we will together rebuild our society on a stronger foundation.

FORREST CHURCH
New York City
September 30, 2001

Invocation

‹«← →»›

Robert Lee Hill

*The Reverend Bob Hill, senior minister of Church of Christ,
Kansas City, Missouri, was on sabbatical at the time of the
terrorist attack. He wrote this poem, "Will and Testament,"
the following morning and then drove to New York City.*

This morning is definitively different,
and thus it seems only meet and right so to do:
to say it out loud:

I will make the bed,
and then I will make coffee,
and then I will play with the cats,
and then I will make an appointment
with my dermatologist
regarding that oblong splotch on my arm.

I will read the paper,
and then I will write my brother,
and then I will bless my mother and my father,
and then I will pray for my two sisters and
   their families,

as their children get themselves and their
    questions ready
for Sunday School next weekend.

I will visit neighbors
with green peppers and the last of this year's
    ripe tomatoes,
and then I will bake cookies
for the firefighters down on Wornall Road (and
    everywhere),
and then I will—with deliberate and
    determined joy—walk
down the Brookside exercise trail.

I will read E. L. Doctorow's *City of God*,
and then I will buy one Valencia orange,
and then I will devour several of Priscilla's
    divine brownies,
and then I will light three candles in the
    cathedral,
as a sign of what will be, what can be, what is
truly worthy today and for any welcoming
    tomorrow.

I will work with my hands in the yard,
and then I will wash my hands thoroughly,
and then I will look out our healing kitchen
    window,
and then I will drink two glasses of water,
and then I will thirst for some new day
and some new, saving strangers to come into
    our town.

I will sit in my cherished chair,
and I will listen to rain, rumbling,
and I will write a preamble for the new
    constitution

and bi-laws for the Harmony Center,
and, with all defiance, I will make plane
    reservations for Seattle,
dreaming of Orcas Island.

I will call out to Willa,
all three-foot-high, seven years old of her,
across the street, and to Miles,
her burgeoning little brother, too,
and I will honor the sheer testament of grace
    that they are
in the arms of their parents in this world.

I will drive down my favorite expressway,
and then I will eat the world's greatest
    barbecue at Gates,
and then I will remember Martin King
and Martin Buber and Martin Luther
and Martina Navratilova,
and then I will testify of a need for still more
    saints.

I will laugh once today, at the very least,
and then I will remember Robert Frost
and then I will recall Emily Dickinson's
    late-coming fame,
and then I will change the oil in my Jeep,
and then I will take my Ansel Adams photos of
    Manzanar
to the frame shop.

I will write a check for the United Negro
    College Fund,
and then I will barter for season tickets
for the rest of the Chiefs' schedule, and
    beyond,
and then I will contact the cemetery in

Groesbeck, Texas,
about the marker for Lewis,
and then I will open the screen porch for the
    evening sun to come in.

I will call up Emanuel,
and then I will testify to Thomas,
and then I will offer a bowl of oranges to
    Buddha,
and then I will have hope with Paul,
and then I will seek Muhammad's mountain.
and then I will purchase a plot with Jeremiah.

I will ring a bell,
and then I will climb a hill,
and then I will sing a song (very loud),
and then I will recite Psalm 22,
and then I will cry with all anguish
the cry of those of us who are not dead.

On this definitively different day, I will do all
    these things
and I will do even more tomorrow,
and I will say it out loud again, until they hear
    it, until I hear it, clearly.

Wednesday,
September 12

Lighting Candles

Against the Darkness

When the World Becomes a Nightmare

R. Scott Colglazier

*The Reverend R. Scott Colglazier, senior minister of
University Christian Church, Fort Worth, Texas, preached
these words at a Wednesday evening memorial service. The
author of several spiritual guidebooks, he has recently edited an
ecumenical volume of peace sermons entitled,* Yes to Peace.

ON TUESDAY MORNING, SEPTEMBER 11, 2001, the
world became a nightmare. As a nation we looked
on with horror as hijacked airliners were turned into
destructive missiles, crashing into the World Trade
Center in New York City, the Pentagon in Washington, D.C., and the countryside of rural Pennsylvania.

Tonight there are no words that can adequately
describe what we have seen the past few days on our
television sets and have read about in our daily
newspapers. As American citizens who are Christian,
Jewish, Buddhist, Hindu, and, yes, Muslim, we are
stunned, staggered, and shocked. Tonight is a night for
prayer and mourning.

Comparisons have been made to that day of "infamy" in our national history, the attack on Pearl Harbor in 1941. However, the differences between that day and the events of these last hours are striking. Moreover, the differences only add to our dismay as Americans. At least we knew then who the enemy was, who perpetrated the attack, and at least it was a military installation that was targeted years ago in the Pacific.

But what happened in New York City and Washington, D.C., is a vivid reminder that the face of war has changed. It was terrorists who drove a stake through the heart of America. Not another country declaring war and invading our shores, but terrorists who have chosen to make absolute their view of the world, deciding that any means justifies their undefined end, including the means of death and destruction. Part of the vulnerability we are feeling as a nation is not just the fear of war, but our fear of an ever-shifting, amorphous threat.

This is a time to pray for our nation, not out of a shallow, clichéd patriotism, but as people who are mourning. Perhaps more than any other time in our storied national history do we need the healing and wisdom of God. That's why we pray for fellow citizens who have lost their lives. We pray for the courageous Americans who are leading rescue efforts. We pray for our president as he carries the heavy burden of leadership. We pray for Congress as they deliberate upon critical next steps for our nation's future.

But we are also in this great house of worship tonight because we need spiritual guidance. Some of us may be asking, "Where was God? How could God let this happen? If God didn't protect the innocent lives of our fellow citizens, how can I believe God will protect me and my family?" These questions take enormous courage to ask, but to ask them is not an indication of a lack of faith—just the opposite—they represent the best of faith. All you have to do is leaf through the Bible, and what you will discover is that people throughout the centuries have found the courage to ask such questions.

I want to suggest that God can be found in the face of our suffering nation. Not the kind of God who causes suffering. Not the kind of God who even allows suffering. But the kind of God who works within the complexities of human life, always trying to inspire people to goodness and justice and compassion. But even as God tries to inspire this, God also risks human rejection. The stark truth of God is this: God invites people to be good, but God cannot make people be good, because the minute someone is made to be good, it is no longer goodness. Therefore, as we see the shocking images and hear the human stories of suffering, we can take consolation that God is not above it, anymore than God is the cause of it. God is living the nightmare with us.

But it also needs to be said tonight that God can be found in the face of compassion. The nightmare is real, but people of faith affirm that hope and compassion are also real. We may never know how many terrorists were on those four airliners, but the number of terrorists will surely pale in comparison to the overwhelming number of police officers and firefighters and emergency workers who responded to human need with human compassion. And if that's not enough to convince us that God is still at work within the human family, all we have to do is think of the doctors and nurses and chaplains and Red Cross workers and city and national leaders, volunteers lined up for hours just waiting to donate blood. God is in the face of hope and compassion.

This is a time for people of every religious persuasion to become people of understanding. We must understand, now more than ever, the difference between vengeance and justice, the difference between fundamentalist extremists and people of ethnicity and genuine religious practice, and we must understand that we don't fight hate with hate. We fight hate with understanding and reason and justice. These are the basic human values embodied in the ideals of our democracy as well as our faith in God. This horrific attack on America cannot shatter America any more than this tragedy can shatter our faith in God, because who we are as Americans is too strong, and who we are as men and women of faith is too resilient.

Offer your prayers tonight. Give thanks for the goodness of the human spirit in spite of the smoldering rubble and the loss of life tonight. Remember those who are suffering tonight. Pray for our world and the human family. We have such a long way to go. And pray for the children and teenagers of our nation who are feeling so utterly vulnerable.

Years ago the poet Theodore Roethke wrote, "In a dark time, the eye begins to see." This is a dark time for America. But perhaps it will be true that in a dark time, the heart will begin to pray.

The Wake of Terror

Forrest Church

This sermon was preached at a candlelighting vigil held at All Souls Unitarian Church in New York City thirty-four hours after the first plane struck the World Trade Center. Fully half of the eight hundred mourners lit candles in memory of their fallen neighbors, loved ones, and friends.

HOW PRECIOUS LIFE IS AND HOW FRAGILE. We know this as we rarely have before, deep within our bones we do. I am not certain how much more we know right now. Our minds imprinted with templates of horror, our hearts bereft with truly unimaginable loss, we face a newly uncertain future. The signposts have all been blown away.

I am so grateful to see you, each and every one. How profoundly we need one another, especially now, but more than just now. We are not human because we think. We are human because we care. All true meaning is shared meaning. The only thing that can never be taken from us is the love we give away.

So let me begin simply by saying, "I love you." I love your tears and the depths from which they spring.

I love how much you want to *do* something, anything, to make this all better. We all feel helpless right now; I know that. At times like these and today uniquely so, in the midst of our daily stroll through life, reality leaps out from behind the bushes and mugs us. How I ache for those of you who have lost dear friends and loved ones to this senseless and barbaric act of terror. How I ache for all of us, who awakened this morning to a new skyline, not only here in New York, but all across America.

The future as we know it is dead. Long after the smoke clears from lower Manhattan and the banks of the Potomac, our vision will be altered by the horror of September 11. No longer can we measure human accomplishment by technological mastery or by our standard of living. Henceforth, for years at least, we shall be remembered by two things above all others, one conveniently ignored, the other too often forgotten over decades devoted to material progress. Unmistakably and forever inoculated against innocence by this full-scale outbreak of terrorism's virus on our own shores, as a nation we shall be known by the steadiness of our resolve in leading the war against the perpetrators and sponsors of terrorism all around the globe.

And as individuals, truly now members of one embattled body, we shall be known no longer by the symbols of abundance and prosperity, but by how well we learn to recognize our own tears in one another's eyes. Hope will answer helplessness if, and only if, from the sacrament of this shared sacrifice of innocence and the innocent, we become channels for one another through which our faith may flow, and wells of love from which to draw much-needed comfort and new strength.

At first these visions of a future rebuilt upon yesterday's ashes may seem to contradict one another. Justice and mercy. Anger and compassion. War and love. Yet they will only be at odds should we choose one vision in place of the other. On the one hand, if hatred and vengeance spur a lust for retribution, rather than the greater quest for peace, we will but add to the world's terror even as we seek to end it. On the other, if we pray only for peace, we shall surely abet the spread of terrorism. Our hands will end up far bloodier than those that lift up arms against it.

History supports each of these statements. In the first instance, we must recall history's most ironic lesson: *Choose your enemies carefully, for you will become like them.* Terrorism is powered by hatred. If we answer the hatred of others with hatred of our own, we and our enemies will soon be indistinguishable. It is hard, I know, to curb the passion for vengeance. When we see Palestinian children dancing in the street to celebrate the slaughter of our neighbors and loved ones, how can we help but feel a surge of disgust and anger, the very emotions that precipitate hatred? But the Palestinians are not our enemy. Nor are the Muslims. This is not, as some historians would have it, a war between civilizations. It is a war between civilization and anarchy, a war of God-demented nihilists against the very fabric of world order. I hope you will all go out of your way in the days ahead to practice the second great commandment and love your Arab neighbors as yourself. Few outside the circle of those who lost loved ones in yesterday's tragedy are more surely its victims than are the millions of innocent Muslims whose God's name has been taken so savagely in vain.

This said, to pray only for peace right now is unwittingly to pray for a war more unimaginable than awakening to the World Trade Center smoldering in ashes. After a day's worth of breathless repetition, we may be tiring of the Pearl Harbor metaphor, even finding it dangerous. Yet, if anything, the comparison is too comforting. After simmering for decades, yesterday war commenced in earnest against an enemy more elusive and more dangerous than any we have ever known before. Good people here in America and around the world must join in a common struggle against a common foe. The only way the world as we know it will not end in a chaos of nuclear terror is if we take every appropriate measure to subdue the threat of terrorism.

Both challenges are daunting. I am not in the least confident that success in either or both will prove possible. And I know that the effort to curb terrorism will shed more innocent blood, claiming the precious and fragile lives of children and parents, lovers and friends, falling from windows, crushed under buildings. But the future as we knew it ended yesterday. Even as Churchill not Chamberlin answered the threat of Hitler, we must unite to respond to this new threat with force not appeasement.

With the war to be fought one between civilization and anarchy, our only hope lies in the balance we strike as we enter this uncertain and forbidding future. It rests in how well we balance justice and mercy, retribution and compassion, the might of weapons and the power of love. Our hope hinges on how effectively we unite a riven world against an elusive enemy. But it also requires that, singly and together, we answer the challenge of maturity that will arise so quickly from the ashes of our shattered innocence. To do this we must not only gird our minds; we must also prepare our hearts. Above all else, this is a spiritual challenge, one that each one of us must meet. If before we could seemingly afford the luxury of relegating our spiritual lives to the occasional Sunday, today, facing a transfigured future, we must redirect our energies and spirits. In times like these, measured against the preparation of our souls, all lesser priorities lose their urgency.

The Chinese ideogram for crisis juxtaposes two word-pictures: danger and opportunity. Even as our grief today can be measured by our love, the danger we now face suggests a commensurate opportunity. When the word *crisis* is used in the theater, it doesn't point to some terrible occurrence, but rather to the quandary that follows. In Greek the word *crisis* means "decision." In the wake of this tragedy, it is the decisions we make that will shape our character and (to a degree) drive the plot our lives will follow.

If religion is our human response to being alive and having to die, the purpose of life is to live in such a way that our lives will prove worth dying for. Over the past two days, all of us have lived with a heightened sense of life's preciousness and fragility. We know how easily it could have been us right now for whom some dear one was about to light a candle. Yet the same thing that makes us more attentive to death can also bring us to life. This saving opportunity matches the danger we have witnessed and now feel. And we are just entering the period of crisis.

The survivors in this city, every one of us, have been changed by this tragedy and will continue to be changed by the decisions we make over the days and years ahead. We can decide to be angry, vengeful, hateful, becoming like our enemies and poisoning the one well. We can also decide that we can't do anything—that the world is hopeless—and go back to our trivial pursuits as if tomorrow were no different than the day before yesterday. Or we can rise to the challenge and pledge our hearts to a higher calling. We can answer to the better angels of our nature and join in a shared struggle, not only against our foes—who are the world's foes—but also on behalf of our friends and neighbors. We can listen more attentively for the voice of God within us than ever before. We can heed its urgings with acts of kindness and deeds of love.

This is already happening. It is happening here this evening. It has been happening on every street corner of this great and newly compassionate city, from sacraments of self-forgetting valor to the redemptive mingling of tears. Though our minds have been singed forever by imprints of horror, our hearts join in deep admiration for the ordinary courage and simple goodness of our neighbors, made one in shared suffering, reminding each other of how splendid we can truly be.

Never forget this. Never forget the e-mail sent by a doomed employee in the World Trade Center, who, just before his life was over, wrote the words, "Thank you for being such a great friend." Never forget the man and woman holding hands as they leapt together to their death. Pay close attention to these and every other note of almost unbearable poignancy as it rings amid the cacophony. Pay attention and then commit them to the memory of your heart. For though the future as we knew it is no longer, we now know that the very worst of which human beings are capable can bring out the very best. From this day forward, it becomes our common mission to be mindful of both aspects of our nature: to counter the former while aspiring to the latter; to face the darkness and yet redeem the day.

In this church there are no easy answers. But after yesterday, easy answers too are part of the past. What our future holds is uncertain, but of this I am sure. What brings us together can hold us together. If together we live in such a way that our deaths, and those whose deaths have changed us, prove worth dying for, we shall (if God exists) have answered God's prayers.

Friday,
September 14

❧❧

Muslim Prayers for Peace

We Will Never Be the Same

Talib W. 'Abdur-Rashid

*Imam Al-Hajj Talib W. 'Abdur-Rashid is the spiritual
leader of the Mosque of Islamic Brotherhood in Harlem,
where he preached these words at a weekly prayer service. He
is also the chairman of the justice committee of the Islamic
Leadership Council of New York, and the deputy leader of
the Muslim Alliance in North America.*

THE ATTACKS UPON THE WORLD TRADE CENTER
and Pentagon this past week are events that have
been permanently branded upon the consciousness of
the American people. Life will never be the same for us
all again. People throughout the city and nation are
hurt, grieving, and confused. They are filled with a
tremendous sadness and sense of loss, magnified by
despair. As a Muslim religious leader in this city, I
have listened to phone calls; some of them angry, pro-
fane, and threatening; others pained but compassionate and supportive.

Walking the eerily deserted streets of lower Manhattan these past few days, I witnessed blank and
dazed stares in the eyes of many folk, reflecting shock,
disbelief, unanswered questions, fear, and uncertainty.

I have talked with people of various ethnicities, stood in houses of worship in the presence of Christians, Jews, Muslims, and others, and watched many people weep as they try to comprehend how such wanton destruction of life and property could occur.

This is a moment of trial for everyone. Almighty Allah has stated in the Qur'an, "Every soul shall have a taste of death." The truth of these words is often difficult to bear, but the words also express an undeniable reality. At this moment, none of us has any way of knowing the identity of all of the victims here in New York, or in Washington. We can all be sure, though, that they will prove to be of all racial and ethnic groups, and of various religions including that of Al-Islam. Some fifteen hundred Muslims worked in the World Trade Center and its immediate surrounding area. They worshiped in a large loft nearby, and even in a room in the World Trade Center itself.

Muslims constituted at least 25 percent of the restaurant workers of Local 100 employed in the Windows on the World Restaurant. They were employed in the trade center complex in various capacities from financiers to porters, and hot dog vendors to office workers. They are gone now, along with their fellow workers of other faiths.

We grieve for our lost loved ones, and empathize with all people suffering loss. Yet even as we extend our condolences, we also counsel ourselves and others to patience, restraint, and tolerance. America preaches faith and tolerance daily. Now, even as the government prepares for a measured response to the attacks, our deeds must match our preaching.

Timothy McVeigh was raised as a Roman Catholic. But when his identity was revealed no one blamed the Catholic Church for his sins. No one attacked Catholics. No one vilified a faith or blamed its adherents for the deeds of a minority. Even if he had said that his motivation was religious, few would have believed it. So it must be with Muslims and Al-Islam.

This week, Muslim leaders have received reports of random attacks upon men and women of our faith in various cities: New York, Cleveland, Hartford, Connecticut, and Detroit. Some of the victims were beaten; others killed by gun shots or stabbings. Further, people of other faiths such as Sikhs, have been attacked right here in New York City, by people mistaking them for Arabs or Muslims or both. On Friday September 14, a group of Christians was harassed on Fourteenth Street simply because they were praying and calling for peace. Their abusers were people calling for revenge.

Thus we see common people assigning guilt by association of religion or ethnicity to others, and expressing their understandable grief and rage by attacking those who are themselves innocent of any wrongdoing. This must stop. For too long the American people have preached to the peoples of the world that the joy of life lies only in the "American Way."

Likewise, we have stood apart from the grief and suffering of our brothers and sisters in the human family, living elsewhere. Thus, too many of us have been collectively uninterested in the effect of American foreign policy on simple people like ourselves. We have been oblivious to their pain.

As others in various countries have suffered daily loss of lives, experiencing grief, tragedy, and destruction of property at the hands of men, we in this country have gone about living our lives in relative prosperity, isolated from their suffering or seeing it as unrelated to us. This too must stop.

Let all people of faith cope with the aftermath of this tragedy by seeking divine help through patient perseverance and prayer. We must humbly open our hearts to all people and encourage others to do the same. For the arrogant and haughty shall be brought low by the one who created us all. Let us pray, then work, for genuine reconciliation of human conflict through a pursuit of true justice for all people, guided by the higher principles we all hold dear.

Sunday,
September 16

The Christian Sabbath:
One Light, Many Windows

Fear Itself

Jim Somerville

*The Reverend Dr. Jim Somerville is pastor of the First
Baptist Church of the City of Washington, D.C. An often
anthologized preacher, he also teaches in the religion
department at Wingate University.*

A T ABOUT 8:45 A.M. ON SEPTEMBER 11, an airplane slammed into the North Tower of the
World Trade Center. We thought it was an accident: a
malfunction in a navigational computer that had re-
sulted in the unthinkable. But then, twenty minutes
later and while many of us were watching it live on television, a second airplane slammed into the South
Tower, erupting in a ball of flame. At that moment we
realized it couldn't be an accident. We realized that
this was a deliberate act of aggression, an attack on the
United States. Thirty-five minutes later we heard that
a third plane had crashed into the Pentagon, just
across the river, and then the rumors began to fly. The
telephone in my office rang with a report that smoke
was pouring out of the Old Executive Office Building.

In the hallway someone said that a car bomb had exploded outside the State Department. One of the teachers in our child development center asked, "Is it true that the Washington Monument is . . . gone?" It seemed that the whole city, the whole nation, was under violent attack.

When things got a little quieter, we opened the church to those who might want to pray and watched as streams of people headed up Sixteenth Street from downtown. Traffic was snarled, the Metro was jammed, and so they walked. Some stopped in to say a brief prayer, but most of them hurried by with their heads down, determined to get home to their families and to get away from the threat of danger. By 3:00 P.M. Washington looked like a ghost town. We closed the doors and started home on empty streets in eerie silence.

In the days since then we have been trying to assess the damage, both physical and emotional. We know that the Pentagon has a gaping hole in its side and the World Trade Center is gone forever. We know that thousands of people have died in this attack, most of them horribly. And we know that we feel shaky and scared, straining our ears for the sounds of airplanes, jumping at every strange or sudden noise.

It is an evil thing that has happened, and it is a particular kind of evil.

Theologians speak of the suffering that human beings experience as a result of earthquake, famine, fire, and flood as *natural evil.* The other kind, which Daniel Migliore describes as the "suffering and evil that sinful human beings inflict on each other and on the world they inhabit," is called *moral evil.* The evil we have experienced in this attack on America is of that latter, darker kind. It has been inflicted upon us. As much as we might suffer from natural evil, this other kind of evil is worse, because it comes not from the violent yet innocent forces of nature, but from the evil intentions of the human heart.

Some people have asked me how God could allow such a thing to happen. Why did he not divert those planes at the last moment? It is the same sort of question people ask when a hurricane pounds the coast, but the answer is different. In cases such as those we say that we live in a world where hurricanes happen, and that sometimes populated coastlines get in the way. It doesn't mean that the hurricane itself is evil, but only that the meeting between high winds and fragile buildings can produce tragic results. But in cases like this one, we have to say that we live in a world where God has given people freedom. The same freedom that allows us to choose God and serve God allows others to hijack planes and bring down buildings. Freedom itself is good. The use some make of that freedom is evil. So, why didn't God intervene? Why didn't God divert those airplanes and save those lives? Because freedom itself was at stake, and God cannot take away our freedom to choose evil without also taking away our freedom to choose good. He would end up with a world of grinning puppets, dancing dumbly at the end of their strings, capable of neither love nor hate. God doesn't want children like that any more than you do. And so—like a mother who sobs as her son is convicted of murder—he watches buildings collapse while his own heart breaks, and wraps his arms around a broken nation.

Franklin D. Roosevelt said the only thing we have to fear is fear itself, but he wasn't talking about what happened last Tuesday. He wasn't talking about what happens when people use their God-given freedom to rain down horror on others. And yet there is a sense in which he was right. Fear isn't the only thing we have to fear, but it is the most formidable of the weapons that have been turned against us in recent days. While a terrorist might use an airplane or a bomb to accomplish his purpose, his purpose, ultimately, is to *terrify*, to bring a nation to its knees by means of fear itself. And to the extent that we are terrified, he has succeeded.

Whoever is behind last Tuesday's attacks hopes that you and I will become too afraid to function. He wants us to tremble with fear every time an airplane passes overhead. He wants us to jump at every strange or sudden noise we hear. He wants to bring us to that place where we will not go to work in the morning or send our children to school. That is why I doubt that the attack on America is over. The nature of terrorism is to keep us off balance, to make us think that death could be waiting for us around the next corner or behind the next tree. The goal of terrorism is to overthrow a nation by paralyzing its people with fear. When we reach that point, the terrorist has won, and I, for one, don't intend to give him that satisfaction.

I refuse to be afraid.

The writer of Psalm 23 claims that even as he is walking through the valley of the shadow of death, he will fear no evil. Not natural evil. Not moral evil. Why? Because God is with him. In these familiar, well-worn words we have the antidote to fear. God's presence is what will make it possible for us to walk through this shadowy valley without being afraid. That doesn't mean we won't listen for the sound of airplanes passing overhead. It doesn't mean we won't jump when we hear a strange or sudden noise. It only means that we will hold tight to God's hand and go on with our lives—that we will refuse to be afraid.

A Mighty Fortress Is Our God

Stephen Bauman

The Reverend Stephen Bauman is senior minister of Christ Church United Methodist in New York City. He also has served as chair of the Foundation for Community Encouragement, organized by M. Scott Peck and others committed to overcoming the barriers to effective human communication.

Among the rubble of this week was the language meant to capture the height, length, breadth, and depth of the catastrophe. No words I heard on the news reports were adequate for the occasion. A variety of commentators likened it to one more circle of Dante's hell, a revisited Mount St. Helens, a nuclear winter, the edge of a crater of a volcano. One said it was bigger than the *Hindenburg,* bigger than the *Titanic.* Pearl Harbor was invoked repeatedly, but no phrase this week has come close to Roosevelt's "day of infamy" back then.

Our language has become so impoverished in this age of hyperbole; vapid popular culture has so overwhelmed our consciousness that we lack an adequate vocabulary to express the size of our experience. One of the reasons so many people have showed up at church for so many worship services for so many days is to help fill this language void. Having no words of their own, hearing no words large enough on television, they seek out those places that might have at least some words that can give expression to their anguish and battered hope.

So we have relied mightily on the ancient poetry of Psalms, the proclamation of prophets, and the testimony of disciples this week to give voice to the groans of our souls. And it has helped. No doubt many stepped into a church for the first time in a long time in the past few days and found a word or two that spoke for them.

Still, words can take us only so far into the depth of our experience. I was acutely aware of this as I thought about what might be said today. I imagined all the possible scenarios around the nation, all the ministers stepping into their pulpits, trying to find words that could reach the deep places in the hearts of their anxious listeners. I wondered how I might get out of my own way up here so that something truthful could be communicated, something authentic, something that wasn't simply cleverly disguised religious hyperbole that went down relievedly, even delightfully easy this morning, yet failed to sate the real hunger by mid afternoon.

What has occurred to me is that what I really have to offer in this short time are a few simple words concerning several basic truths. They're things we *might* have known once a long time ago, way back before last Tuesday, but now we're not certain we ever really knew them. So the few words I have speak of simple matters. But don't for a moment equate simple with shallow. Instead think of simple as foundational, bedrock; as essential to life; as the ground we walk upon, the air we breathe.

I have just three simple things to say today and each is only two words long. You might think of these as the three essentials of our faith. In the weeks ahead you will want to travel down the spiritual paths they open, but for now, if you were to jot them down on a slip of paper and stick them in the corner of your bathroom mirror or attach them on the refrigerator door where you see them every day, you will have relearned the essential catechism of the Christian faith, and not as some esoteric system of religious mumbo jumbo, but as the truest, most important things you know.

The first two words I have are these: *God is*. When our lives are struck hard by crisis, our usual supports are rent asunder. Things we've taken so for granted, matters we've assigned principle importance are exposed as less significant than we thought. All of a sudden life seems out of control, chaotic. We lose our bearings, become disoriented. Didn't that happen to most of us this week? Didn't you find it hard to concentrate? To maintain a sense of proportion and balance in your life? Doesn't it seem as though the world you thought you knew a week ago has shifted out of focus? Did it ever really exist at all?

If you've ever been in a sizable earthquake you know of an instinctual terror of the loss of the very ground you walk upon. But that lasts only for a few seconds. The sigh of blessed relief when the tremors pass indicates that everything is as it once was. But what happens when everything isn't as it once was, as we now fear is the case? What then?

Then we shift our attention to a ground that lies even deeper. The scriptures of our tradition help us here. Indeed, that is their essential purpose. They provide an ancient library of the recurring human discovery that *God is*. That behind all things lies a fundamental order. That's why people flocked to churches this week. They needed to remember something they thought they once knew. And so the scriptures were opened and people found resonance with ancient poetry: "Have you not known? Have you not heard? The Lord is the everlasting God, the Creator of the ends of the earth. He does not faint or grow weary. . . . Those who wait for the Lord shall renew their strength, they shall mount up with wings like eagles, they shall run and not be weary, they shall walk and not faint" (Isa. 40:28–31).

We know these words were forged in the crucible of great human adversity and tragedy. For millennia people confronted with great crises have seen behind and beneath their experience a more fundamental order and others who then followed learned the wisdom of their forebears that *God is*.

My second words are these: *God loves*. Something that has struck me powerfully this week is that when stripped of our mundane preoccupations, we quickly identify the importance of our relationships with one another, especially those closest relationships that give shape and meaning to our lives. If I were to ask for a show of hands of those who called the people they loved this week simply to touch base, simply to say, "I love you," there would be hardly a hand that wouldn't go up.

Some of the most deeply affective moments I had this week came on Tuesday in the few minutes of conversation I had with my son and daughter away at college. Each conversation ended with, "I love you." "I love you too." These simple words spoken with a depth and eloquence in those moments that Shakespeare himself could not have written.

Why is this? Why is this our instinct, as opposed to some other behavior? It would seem that this deep connection, this profound instinct for loving relationship is among the most elemental human characteristics. We are evidently designed for loving relationships. That we seem so poor at its execution provides material for a lifetime of sermons. For today, we need simply to acknowledge this truth, *to see it clearly*—maybe for the first time in a very long time. Is it the stock portfolio? The house? Career? Anything else you could name that is of more primary importance?

There is a phrase in one of our Gospels that goes like this: "God so loved the world that he gave his only begotten Son" (John 3:16). That same Son said that the primary mission in life is the sentence we have in our mosaics above the altar: To love God with all of our heart, soul, mind, and strength, and to love our neighbor as ourselves. Love is the essential life energy. It is the essential verb in a meaningful life. And as our tradition instructs, this is no sentimental matter. This holy love is acquainted with grief and sorrow. It knows desperation and loss. Didn't Jesus cry out on the cross in a lonely despair, seemingly abandoned by his friends and, for a moment, even by God himself?

And yet, this leads to my last two words: *God saves*. In the face of evident disaster, God wrought victory. Did you know that every Sunday is in fact a mini resurrection celebration? Did you know that we're doing something here today that flies in the face of what the terrorists intend? Their intention is to strip us of a confident hope. That's what the power of hate wants to accomplish. Hate is a destroyer. Love builds up. Hate feeds on fear. Love feeds on hope. If we have even a smidgen of hope, we have been touched by grace. Hope is the engine of God's salvation. Hope is the fruitful acknowledgment that *God is* and that *God loves*. Hope instructs that love is stronger even than death itself. That's the deep message at the heart of authentic Christian faith.

Hope is what led Paul to ask, "Who will separate us from the love of Christ? Will hardship, distress, persecution, famine, nakedness, peril, sword? . . . I am convinced that neither death, nor life, nor angels, nor rulers, nor things present, nor things to come, nor powers, nor height, nor depth, nor anything else in all creation will be able to separate us from the love of God" (Rom. 8:35–39). That is God's salvation.

There are some questions we cannot adequately answer in this life, chief among them is why suffering and evil exist in our world. But here are three things we can claim in response to the suffering and evil: *God is, God loves,* and *God saves.*

Brotherly Love

Daniel W. Murphy

The Reverend Daniel W. Murphy, a Roman Catholic priest,
is pastor of Blessed Kateri Tekawitha Parish in Sparta,
New Jersey. Father Murphy's youngest brother, Edward,
forty-two, of Clifton, New Jersey, was one of the victims of
the World Trade Center tragedy. He worked as a
commodities trader for Cantor Fitzgerald.

I REALLY DEBATED WHERE I SHOULD BE TODAY. Should I be at home in Clifton with my family, or should I be here with you, my other family? During most of my twenty-eight years as a priest, I have been the one who is called upon to bring comfort, compassion, meaning, and hope to others in a time of loss, preaching the Christian message, which proclaims that from death comes life. Now, I have to really believe that deeply in my heart. So, who besides me is better able to speak with you today, as we look for hope, meaning, and some ray of light in the face of this horror and tragedy?

The gospel stories today speak so beautifully of being lost and being found. As a Christian people this is the core of what we are all about. Every time we gather at that table of the Eucharist, we proclaim, "Christ has died, Christ has risen, Christ will come again." We believe that from death, as tragic and terrible and unforeseen as it might be, life comes forth. No matter what is lost, something is always found. Where do we find life? What do we find amid all of this loss?

So many people this week have come up to me and said, "Dan, you must be so filled with anger." And I respond to them, saying, "Believe it or not, I have absolutely no anger in my heart." Maybe in time, as a part of my grief process, that might come. But I feel no anger.

I feel a tremendous sadness to have lost my youngest brother. I feel a tremendous sense of pain for my mom who has lost her youngest son, her "baby." My brother was single and had a very vibrant, active life. He lived only a few blocks from my mom, and he was there every day. So I feel my mother's pain. Anger, no.

Yes, we need to act to end terrorism. But we cannot allow our hearts to be filled with hatred, anger, and revenge. History teaches us that revenge builds upon revenge, and more revenge. It never ends. Yes, we need to seek justice. But we need to seek a justice based not on hatred or anger over what has happened, but rather out of concern for the future of all the human community.

My other brother, Richie, and I shared this week how many wonderful Arab friends we have in our own lives. Growing up in Clifton, there were always Arabs in our midst. At my first assignment in Wayne, we had a large number of Arabs in our parish, and to me they are among the warmest, kindest, and most outreaching people I have ever met. I have met many Muslims. Muslims are a people with a great faith in God, a deep focus.

The other night I took a long walk to spend time alone and, to be honest, to cry. Walking near my mom's house I saw a big pickup truck with bright lights blaring and the sound system going as loud as it could. It was festooned with American flags and on the back of the truck was a big sign that read, "Kill all those damn Arabs and fry them all!" My first instinct when I came up to him was to tap him on the shoulder and say, "Buddy, can I share a story with you? Can I let you know where I am coming from and how I could never put that sign on my car?" Then I stopped. I thought perhaps this man was sharing in the same pain that I have. Perhaps this is the only way, at this point, that he could respond.

When I see all these flags everyone is waving or wearing, I hope and I pray they are symbols of our solidarity, our union as a nation, in grieving and in reaching out in love and compassion to those who have suffered loss. And I hope and I pray that I can have peace when I know that many of those flags express anger, hatred, and vengeance. Do these flags just symbolize our belief that our strength lies in military power and high-tech weapons?

St. Paul tells us, "God's grace, God's love is abundant." The beautiful stories of the lost coin and the lost sheep and the prodigal son speak of an extravagant love. The word "prodigal" means extravagant. It refers far more to the father than it does to the son.

One day this week as I came back to the parish to pick up some things to take back to Clifton, I drove up the driveway and saw a huge number of boxes and black bags. When I asked what all those boxes were for, I was told that they were the outpouring of love for the rescue workers, the people and even the dogs. My heart was so deeply touched to see a truck donated by one of our parishioners, to see teenagers loading boxes to express our love for the people.

That is the power that we have as an American people. Our power is not in guns or high-tech weapons or military forces. It is in the extravagant love of God. Is this not a countercultural message? But don't I have the right to speak that message? Because I hurt deeply. I have lost a brother. And yet my faith, and hopefully the faith of all of us, testifies that it is God's abundant love that is the strength of our country, not military power, or military might, or tools of de-struction.

Life is too precious to be consumed by anger and hatred. My brother's life is too precious for me to be ruled by anger, hatred, and feelings of deep revenge.

If you have an American flag outside your house, if you wear an American flag, wear it and display it with pride. But not pride in guns, not pride in bombs or high-tech weapons of revenge. Let it be a source of pride that we can be a people who respond with love, compassion, and healing to end the evil, not only in the terrorists, but the evil and the darkness that exists in every one of us, male and female, young and old. Let it be a symbol of pride that we are a people who have always welcomed the stranger and not shut out those who are different from ourselves.

To Mourn, Reflect, and Hope

Arthur Caliandro

*The Reverend Dr. Arthur Caliandro succeeded Dr. Norman
Vincent Peale as senior minister of Marble Collegiate
Church in New York. For ten years he has also served as
chair of The Partnership of Faith in New York City, an
interfaith group including Muslim, Jewish, Catholic, and
Protestant clergy.*

STORIES. STORIES. Each one of us has stories about
Tuesday and what has happened since. We need to
tell our stories. We need to hear each other's stories.
We, ourselves, are stories.

Tuesday morning at 8:45 A.M., I got out of a taxi here
at the corner of Fifth Avenue and Twenty-ninth
Street. I heard the sound of a jet plane flying very low
overhead. I looked up. I didn't see the plane, but the
sound struck me as odd, because one doesn't hear big
jet planes flying low over Manhattan. It doesn't happen, but this day it did. I gave it no further thought
and I went to my desk. Moments later, my younger
son called me and said, "Dad, get to a television. A
plane just hit the World Trade Center." As he was de-

scribing the scene, he said, "I see another plane coming. It hit the other building! What's going on? Something's happening!"

And it was. And it has.

We've seen those pictures a thousand times since. For generations of Americans, things have changed permanently. For you and for me, things will not be the same again. America has changed permanently. Something has happened.

For thirty years, as I would walk down Fifth Avenue and look straight ahead toward the very bottom tip of Manhattan Island, I would see those two gigantic buildings. And never did I see them without a feeling of awe and wonder that the human mind could create such mammoth, extraordinary structures. I never paused to calculate the immense human loss if all the people who worked in those towers ever became the victims of some attack or calamity. Even with rescue efforts underway today, we still have no way of comprehending just what the toll will be in human loss and pain.

As I look back over the years, I recall that in the first building, building one, there was a restaurant on the 107th floor called Windows on the World. My wife and I would often go there, bringing friends and family members from outside of the city and state. Sometimes we would enjoy special celebrations there. We would look from the south, we would look from the north, we would look from the east, we would look from the west, and see extraordinary views. We felt as if we were seeing the entire world. Those twin towers were the symbol of American free enterprise. They were a symbol of New York and a symbol for the United States.

They were important symbols, like the *Titanic*. But the *Titanic* has sunk again, and with it, thousands of lives have been lost. It's a strange feeling now, coming down Fifth Avenue and not seeing those towers there. I'm still numb. I'm stunned. Where do we look for meaning and answers when we've lost such an important symbol and when people we knew and loved are never going to return?

Time published a special edition on the attack on America, which arrived yesterday. It called those buildings "America's cathedrals." And now the cathedrals are gone. What do we do? Where do we go?

We can go to the wisdom of the ages, the Scriptures, the wisdom of the universe, the word of God. In Psalm 46 we read: "God is in the midst of the city. The city will not be moved. God will help it when the morning dawns."

God is. God has been. God will be. Nobody can destroy the city when God is in the midst of it. We depend on the presence of almighty God. We believe in it and have faith in it. It is an unchangeable, immovable presence.

What else do we do? What must we do for ourselves? Primary, and important—and many people are not likely to do this, but it's essential for our mental health, the health of our communities, the health of the nation—we must take time to mourn and express our grief and our anguish. We must get deeply in touch with our feelings—the feelings of sadness, the feelings of terror, the feelings of fear, the feelings of anxiety. We need to get in touch with our anger. It is important that we get in touch with our feelings, and hold them up and honor them. We need to respect them and give them time and space to do their work. It's important to go deep and get in touch with them.

That is why, on Friday morning, I went to see a therapist.

"Arthur, how are you?" he said. "How are you handling yourself?"

"I'm fine," I said. But I knew inside that I wasn't, and he knew that too. And then I told him how I had built a protective wall around my emotions. I had allowed none of the pain or anguish to get in. I had kept it all outside. I was protecting myself from hurt, from pain, and from feeling.

"Arthur, have you cried?" he asked me.

"No, not really," I said. "There were a couple of times when I started to, but I stopped it right away."

"Tell me about them," he said. "And as you do, cry."

And I said, "I got a call from out of state, from somebody very important to me, in whom I've invested so much of myself. We had become estranged. This person had even refused to take my calls. But that person called after the disaster, and then when I heard that voice—"Arthur, are you all right?"—I started to cry. But I cut it off."

"Cry now," he said. And I did.

"What was the other instance?" he asked.

"This was a strange one for me," I said, "but when I heard that two of the terrorists rented a car in my hometown of Portland, Maine, drove to Boston, and came and did that dastardly thing, that got to me. There are two places that I feel that I belong, that I am passionately in love with—New York City and the coast of Maine—and both were involved, and some-how that got to me."

And I cried in his office. I learned years ago that it's one thing to cry by yourself, but it's very healing to cry in the presence of a significant other person.

"How are you feeling now?" he asked.

"I feel sad—overwhelming sadness," I answered.

And he began to help me explore the sadness, and the other avenues and tributaries of my life where sad-ness exists. I began to discover why these two inci-dents got to me.

And he said, "Arthur, I hope you can stay in this place of sadness." And I have. The sadness is still with me, but identifying the feeling and talking it out has re-lieved some pressure.

Some of you may be feeling sadness. Others of you may be feeling something different. Many of you are feeling intense anger. You're enraged. That's a legitimate feeling. Let it be, and honor it. Only share it with a thoughtful person so that it doesn't get solidified and eventually become destructive.

I have told you a part of my story. You have your story, your journey, your emotions. But please, go down deep, get in touch with the deepest feeling, and let it come out. And give it time. Give it space.

We go again to the Scriptures, to the wisdom of the universe. Jesus said: "Blessed are they that mourn, for they shall be comforted" (Matt. 5:4). What He meant by that is, "You will be made whole again." Jesus also said, "In this world there will be tribulation, but take comfort. I have overcome the world" (John 16:33). And then He said: "In this life you will have pain, but your pain will turn into joy" (John 16:20).

On Wednesday night, I participated in an interfaith service at Fifth Avenue Presbyterian Church, sponsored by the Partnership of Faith, a partnership of Roman Catholic, Protestant, Jewish, and Muslim clergy. There, at the altar of that church, Rabbi Ronald B. Sobel and Shaykh Abd'allah Latif Ali were speaking together in a brotherly embrace. They represent very different backgrounds. There has been so much hostility between faith groups, and yet those two men were together. I have hope, because I have witnessed the beauty and the greatness of the human spirit. We will rise again, and we will be a greater people.

Again we will go to the Scriptures, to the wisdom of the universe, to something that Jesus said to His disciples that we really haven't tried yet. We haven't tried it yet, because we don't believe it really is going to work. But those few individuals who have tried it over the centuries know that it does work, and it makes the difference. Then, and only then, will the world be healed, when we do what we were taught to do when Jesus said to His disciples, "A new commandment I give to you, that you love one another as I have loved you" (John 13:34).

Healing for Lives Touched by Violence

William L. McLennan Jr.

*In his sermon, delivered at Stanford Memorial Church,
the Reverend Scotty McLennan, dean of Religious Life at
Stanford University, addressed the students' anxieties in
very concrete ways. "Don't get glued to your TV. Hold at
least two people a day and let them know they're not alone.
Contribute money. Perform some service to others. Get
politically involved." Here he stresses the saving
power of community.*

OUR LIVES HAVE BEEN CHANGED dramatically, if
not permanently, by the horrendous terrorist violence of last Tuesday. We can't control the feelings
that keep coming: grief, anger, fear, sadness and depression and hopelessness. We want to begin some
kind of healing process, but how can we? It's too soon.
We don't feel safe. There are so many who have died.
So many who have been injured and scarred, physically and emotionally. Some of us have lost family
members and close friends. It's likely that all of us will
be touched personally over the coming days and
weeks as we learn of more and more people, whom we

know, who have suffered grievous loss. Our nation will never be the same again, it seems. Our world has forever changed.

On Friday I listened to a Stanford law student, choked with grief, as he spoke about how he'd lost his college roommate on one of the planes that plowed into the World Trade Center. An education school alumnus walked into my office late in the afternoon to tell me about a classmate who died, Vincent Boland. He'd just graduated from the school of education in June. I returned home in the evening to receive this e-mail from a colleague at Tufts University, where I worked for sixteen years before coming to Stanford earlier this year: "Scotty—I'm not sure if you have gotten the word, but Janet lost her daughter Mary on American Airlines Flight 11 on Tuesday. Mary was Janet's youngest, and as you probably know, they were inseparable. I hope you didn't have any personal losses amid this tragedy. God bless."

The Janet my colleague was speaking of—and I've changed her name to protect her confidentiality—ran the conference bureau for most of my years at Tufts. She was always a wonderful, warm, energetic, optimistic person. Will she ever be the same again?

This is a service of healing for lives touched by violence. How can our Christian faith help us begin the healing process today? For some of us it might come in the powerful music of the Fauré Requiem that you'll be hearing throughout the service, or in the hymns we sing together, or in the glorious strains of our organ. For others it may be through prayer or through joining together in the Holy Eucharist. What comfort, though, can we find in this morning's readings from scripture?

Jesus of Nazareth was a healer, and there are many stories of his healings throughout the New Testament. How did he heal? What did it mean when he healed? How can we be helped, through reading scripture, to begin our own healing process today?

Let's look at the Gospel lesson from Luke. First of all, we're informed that Jesus was teaching one day, inside a house, surrounded by a huge crowd of people. Some men came—four men, to be precise, as we're told in the same story in the book of Mark—carrying a paralyzed man on a bed. We're not informed how he became paralyzed, but we might well imagine today that it was as a result of violence. No doubt he was physically paralyzed, but we might well imagine ourselves today paralyzed by grief or by fear for our safety . . . by depression or hopelessness. The problem, though, was that the four men couldn't maneuver the bed through the crowd and get anywhere near Jesus to ask for healing for their paralyzed friend. But their determination to seek healing was very strong. They managed to get themselves and the bed up onto the roof of the house, they removed a number of tiles, and then they lowered their paralyzed friend on his bed into the middle of the crowd, right in front of Jesus.

"When Jesus saw their faith," he told the paralyzed man to stand up and walk, which he did, "and went to his home, glorifying God" (Luke 5:22–25). Please note that the text says that it was because of the four friends' faith that the paralyzed man was healed. Nothing is said about the man's own faith, and Jesus didn't ask him about his religious beliefs, or his background, or whether he was willing to repent for any particular sins. Jesus just healed him on the spot — no questions asked — as a result of those four friends coming together, taking determined action in service to another, and having the faith that their friend could indeed be healed through the grace of God.

In a nutshell that's the scriptural message for us today, I believe. Three things are needed for healing to begin for each of us, and in this country at large: First, we need to unite in community, rather than feeling isolated and alone, or in some cases scapegoated and attacked for the color of our skin, our national origin, or our religion. Second, we need to take determined action in service to others, getting up off our haunches, no matter how badly we're feeling, rolling up our sleeves, and going to work to rebuild this country and its confidence. Third, we need to have the faith that God will help those who help themselves; we need to have the faith that healing really is possible if we join with others and get moving.

I have a lot of hope for my friend Janet. She always epitomized the values of community, service to others, and faith in God. On campus she seemed to be constantly thinking of ways to get people together — to celebrate birthdays and anniversaries, to help people get to know each other from one far-flung segment of the campus to another, and simply to build Tufts's spirit. She thought big and could organize huge events, seemingly effortlessly. Besides that, she had a great sense of humor and made everyone feel great. She knew the value of community.

In terms of service, I'll never forget one summer when there were terrible drought conditions throughout the Midwest, with lots of farm foreclosures and failing agricultural businesses. Janet started thinking hard about what we could do in Boston. As director of the conference bureau, she controlled a lot of summer dormitory space. So she offered to team up with Catholic Charities and provide housing for members of farming families who would come to Boston to take summer jobs to help get their mothers and fathers or sisters and brothers through a very hard stretch.

And Janet always maintained a quiet but deep faith in God. When she left Tufts, she went down to Atlanta and started working with Habitat for Humanity. She told me that what made her happiest about Habitat, besides the community-building and service they provided, was their explicit commitment to seeing themselves as a Christian ministry. One didn't have to be embarrassed to talk about God at work, even as she and the organization were careful to be inclusive of all, regardless of their religious background or lack thereof. Janet had faith that all things are possible with God.

I can think of very little that's worse than losing one's beloved daughter to terrorism last Tuesday. "Mary was Janet's youngest," my colleague wrote, "and as you probably know, they were inseparable." I doubt there'll be any healing possible in Janet's life this Sunday. Yet, next week, or next month, or certainly by next year, the healing will begin. And it will move into her sinews, and into her bloodstream, and into her heart, and into her very soul. Because I know a community of friends will rally around her in her paralysis. They will lift up the figurative bed on which she is lying, and they will make a determined effort to serve her in whatever way she needs to promote her healing. And since I have an idea of who they are, many of them will act out of their Christian faith that, as the Apostle Paul wrote in his Epistle to the Romans, "neither death, nor life, nor angels, nor principalities, nor powers, nor things present, nor things to come, nor height, nor depth, nor any other creature, shall be able to separate us from the love of God, which is in Christ Jesus our Lord" (Rom. 8:39). As the Gospel lesson this morning teaches, it will be by the faith of her friends that Janet's healing progresses.

Yet, I actually think that's only part of the story. Because I bet that Janet will soon be out there herself building community, as she's always done, in response to this national crisis. She'll be comforting others and working to ensure that no one is abused because they happen to be Muslim or of Middle Eastern descent. She'll be working to channel her own grief and anger, and that of others, into constructive channels of service rather than into hatred and revenge. And she'll be glorifying and praising God, in whom she lives, and moves, and has her being.

It's contagious, this engagement in community, this service to others, and this faith in God. Healing begins with us, though. The paralyzed man would never have been healed in the Gospel story if four men hadn't come together and taken determined action, founded in faith, to see that their friend was given the opportunity to be healed. We need to come together, as we have here today. We need to commit ourselves to bold and sustained action to build a better world. And we need to share our faith in a loving and just God.

Our Refuge and Strength

Joanna Adams

The Reverend Joanna Adams is senior minister of Trinity Presbyterian Church in Atlanta, Georgia. She also serves on the board of directors of the Atlanta Chamber of Commerce.

I HAVE AN AUNT WHO IS WELL INTO THE NINTH decade of her life. Next to her husband and son, both now deceased, her great love has been language. Verses by Elizabeth Barrett Browning and Alfred, Lord Tennyson, have been particular favorites of hers, as well as the poetry of Shakespeare and Shelley. Throughout my childhood, Aunt Sara always had something exquisite to offer in response to an event of great import, until a particularly heartbreaking loss hit our family some years ago. I remember so vividly how she placed her hand over her heart, shook her head, and said to me as her eyes filled with tears, "No words today, Jo. No words today at all."

There are grave moments in life when words seem at the best powerless, or at the very least inadequate.

A friend in another city tells me of how on Tuesday, September 11, when word was breaking of the terrorists' attacks on New York and Washington, a member of his congregation was at home alone. She looked out the window and happened to see the mail carrier at her mailbox. Though he was a new person on the route, a stranger to her, she could think of nothing else to do but to rush down the driveway; wordlessly, the two strangers embraced.

For all of us the shock and loss of the week just past have been too deep for words, and, yet, here we are in church today, needing to begin to make sense of things, yearning to hear a word that would help us respond in faithful, constructive ways to these senseless acts of terrorism and their incalculable consequences in terms of death and human suffering. The great cloud of dust and rubble that rained on the streets and roofs of Manhattan has also dropped its fallout into our souls, cluttering the roads of our reasoning and making our progress out of grief and anger slow and arduous. And, yet, like the brave rescue workers who are making their way through the ruins of the World Trade Center, we must work our way through sorrow and rage, and the only tools we have are words, especially the words of our faith tradition, words that have comforted and healed and offered hope for thousands of years. Their power lies not in eloquence of expression or in mellifluousness of sound, but in the sure spiritual realities that lie beneath them and of which they speak: "I am the resurrection and the life, says the Lord. Those who believe in me, even though they die, shall live, and everyone who liveth and believeth in me shall never die" (John 11:25–26).

"Peace I leave with you, my peace I give unto you, not as the world giveth, give I unto you. Let not your hearts be troubled. Neither let them be afraid" (John 14:27).

"I consider that the suffering of this present day is not worth comparing to the glory that is about to be revealed" (Rom. 8:18).

"Therefore, we will not fear, though the earth should change and the mountains shake at the heart of the sea. The Lord of hosts is with us. The God of Jacob is our refuge" (Psalm 46).

On this Sunday after the Tuesday on which the world was forever changed, we search through the ashes for words, for signs of the invincible promises that still hold the world secure and give us courage to go on. Here they are, as strong as the cedars of Lebanon. The prophet Isaiah put it like this: "The grass withers, the flower fades, but the word of our God will stand forever" (Isa. 40:8). If Isaiah were writing this week, he would have written, "The World Trade Center Towers crumble, the steel girders melt, but the word of our God will stand forever."

It has been said that the opposite of faith is not doubt; often, doubt is a friend to faith. No, the opposite of faith is despair. There is reason aplenty to despair, but the more pressing question is this: Are there reasons to hope? I would submit that there are, and I would like to suggest the following.

First there is the promise we receive by faith that nothing in heaven or on earth can separate us from the love of God made known in Christ Jesus. Second is our trust that the sovereignty of the God of history remains intact. The central conviction of our faith tradition is that actual world history is the locus of God's saving grace, and that the purposes of God can never be finally thwarted by the powers of hate or enmity. I know that it is hard today not to give into cynicism or despair in the face of such suffering, but for the sake of those who have suffered and died, all the thousands of them, we cannot give in. Today more than ever before, we have to be hopeful, loving, wise people. One of you sent me a card this week that had a thought on the front that I have held on to: "He who desires to see the living Lord face to face should not seek him in the empty firmament, but in human love."

My favorite moment in this emotionally heartbreaking week was the spontaneous gathering of members of Congress on the steps of the Capitol, and after they had sung "God Bless America," and as the senators and congressmen started to leave, I saw tall, lanky Trent Lott, conservative Republican Senate leader, put both his big arms around the short Polish liberal Democrat senator Barbara Mikulski. They held on to one another and then walked up the steps arm in arm. Human beings. Americans together.

What more important lesson could we learn from this terrible tragedy than the lesson that life is fragile and that there are more important things than winning—like being united when great calamity threatens? Like being connected by a shared vision of the common good. Like being friends across lines of race, religion, politics, and ideology. Like being family and letting those close to you know how precious they are. Here are a few lines from an e-mail one of you sent to me on Thursday: "If I knew this would be the last time I would see you walk out the door, I would call you back and I would hug and kiss you, and then I would call you back again for one more. And if today is all I get, then I would like to say how much I love you. . . . I'd like to take just a moment to say I am sorry. Please forgive me. Thank you. It is okay. And if tomorrow never comes, then I'll have no regrets about today."

So many have asked what we can do. We can build bridges instead of walls. Is there someone in your life from who you are estranged or against whom you are harboring deep ill will? Try to make peace. Do not let anger get the best of you. I thought about the meaning of that expression yesterday, "Don't let it get the best of you." Think of that literally. The best of you can be eaten away by anger and resentment, and then all we are left with is the hardness of heart and a meanness of spirit out of which nothing good can ever come.

In the weeks ahead our nation is going to need our prayers for moral guidance as never before. We cannot allow the attacks of this past week to go unanswered. Justice demands a strong response, but we must not let a spirit of vengeance get the best of us, so that we ourselves act without regard to innocent lives, that we ourselves betray the great values upon which this country was founded. We must struggle against terrorism with all our wisdom and all our might, but we must never engage in cruel acts of retribution or be motivated by hatred, even toward those who have done evil against us. I wish I didn't even have to say that to you today—I am as angry as you are—but the Gospel says it to us all. This is the hardest part. "Love your enemies, pray for those that persecute you" (Matt. 5:44).

When the allies liberated Ravensbruck, a Nazi death camp, where 92,000 women and children had died, a soldier found this prayer written on a piece of wrapping paper near the body of a dead child: "O Lord, remember not only the men and women of goodwill, but also those of ill will. But do not only remember the suffering they have inflicted on us, remember the fruits we bought—thanks to this suffering, our comradeship, our loyalty, our humility, the courage, the generosity, the greatness of heart which has grown out of all this. And when they come to judgment let the fruits that we have borne be their forgiveness."

And so we must pray for those who persecute us, along with praying that our nation's response will be thoughtful, measured, effective, and just. We must also hope that the coming of God's kingdom is real—real even in the midst of the chaos of history, and more inevitable than the coming of the dawn after the darkness of the night.

At about this hour yesterday, I was sitting at my desk in my study at home, trying but failing to write this sermon. I happened to look out the window just as a great blue heron who lives on our lake sailed in for a morning of fishing. He was so beautiful and graceful, so full of blue heroism. He brought with him the promise that life will go on, the imperative that life must go on lest the evildoers rob us of even more than they have already taken. So still he stood in the shallows, that watching him I picked up my Bible and read aloud these words: "Behold the works of the Lord, who makes wars cease to the ends of the earth. . . . Be still and know that I am God. The Lord of hosts is with us. The God of Jacob is our refuge" (Psalm 46).

Let those words begin to fill your heart and to mend your spirit.

How in God's Name?

Jon M. Walton

*The Reverend Dr. Jon Walton is senior minister of
First Presbyterian Church in New York City, a pastorate
he had just begun when the terrorist attack occurred.
He is the author of a collection of sermons
entitled,* Imperfect Peace.

WHAT WORD IS THERE TO SAY that has not already been said? What cry to heaven has not already been raised that has said so much more than any cry that we might raise? For days this avenue outside our doors was silent, and the silence said it all.

There were screams of sirens, of course, echoes of the screams that came when the Towers fell, the terror of our disbelief that continues to reverberate on the walls of these stone canyons and probably always will. Like the prophet Ezekiel, we now know what he meant when he said, "I sat there among them, stunned, for seven days" (Eze. 3:17).

Like everybody else, deep in my heart, somewhere mixed with all the grieving, there is anger and a rage so deep that it scares even me that I feel it. I know that there is a part of me that wants to get back at the villains, a dark side that would like to send in the troops and open up the bomb bays and reset the missiles for very specific targets. I imagine that with satellites so strong that they can read license plates from miles into the stratosphere that it should be no problem to pinpoint the exact location of the dens of iniquity, the very lairs and hiding places of those who are responsible. I have that in me, I know it, and it is abroad in the land this day, this very worst of blood-thirstiness that is at the heart of our broken nature as sinful people.

And then I catch myself and realize, if we as a people become like those who have banned us, ruthless, lawless, evil, and cunning in our stealth, without care for the lives of innocent human beings whom we dismiss as the inevitable waste of "collateral damage," we will ourselves have allowed evil itself to take over the world, and all the goodness and worthiness that we have as a nation will have been lost in the ghastly plumes of smoke that have risen over us this week.

There were reports at week's end of cruelty and meanness to people of Middle Eastern descent in this nation. And there is graffiti written on telephone kiosks and scrawled on the walls of public places here in the Village threatening harm to Arabs and death to Muslims and my heart sinks at the pity of it! If nothing else, the sight of those towers burning is a symbol to us all of the futility of doing violence to one another in whatever form.

At last it comes down to this, the question that will not stop haunting me day in and day out, that wakes me in the morning and troubles me into the night, the question of how in the name of God such a thing could have been done. How could anyone do this in the name of Allah, or Adonai, or Yahweh, or God Almighty, the Great Mysterious One who is the Creator of Heaven and of Earth. By whatever name you call God, how could anyone imagine that God could be pleased by such a horror? What kind of God is that?

Most assuredly not the God I know. The God I know is a God whose heart was broken Tuesday morning, whose heart has been broken so many times before, who weeps for us, and longs for us to end our warring ways.

The God I know is a God of compassion and love. The God who gave us everything, the earth and the heavens, the sky and the sun, the moon and the stars, and who delighted in it all, and called it good. A God who has given us each other as a blessing to be treasured, who knows us through and through and loves us still and all.

How then, you ask, in God's name, could such a thing happen as this has happened? Could not God have stopped it? Could not God have prevented those zealots from doing the things they did?

And the only thing I can come up with is that God

has been trying. God did not mean for us to have things come out this way.

One thing is for sure, and that is that nothing that I saw on the horizon as I stood out on the sidewalk with everyone else last Tuesday morning looking down Fifth Avenue to those blazing towers at the end of our line of sight . . . nothing that I saw there looked anything like the will of God to me.

To imagine that God intends human suffering, that God wills a terrorist to commandeer a plane and take the lives of thousands of people who were going about a day's work as if it were any other day, is to misunderstand God altogether. God, whose eye is on the sparrow, who has numbered every hair on our head. That was not God's will that I saw there blazing in the sky, that was something quite the opposite.

William Sloane Coffin said on the occasion of his son's death some years ago that, "God's heart was the first of all our hearts to break." And so I think it was again on Tuesday morning, God's heart, that was the first of all our hearts to break. The first to feel the impact of the glass shattering, the first to know the burning of the fire, the first to feel the collapsing of the steel, the first to receive into those everlasting arms the bodies of the wounded and the dying.

I cannot presume to speak for God. No one with such imperfect sight or understanding as we possess on earth can do so. Except to witness to the fact that God has given us One who has taught us a still more excellent way than we have ever yet been able to live. One who has held up to us a better possibility for our living than we have ever yet achieved.

He who took upon himself the pain and suffering and sin of the world, and bore the worst the world could do for the sake of the best that God intended . . . Jesus Christ, in whose name we have gathered today, and by whose love we are drawn together.

In him, we know that the evil of this world will not have the last say. That goodness and mercy and peace shall reign some day, even if not today. That one day, swords will be beaten into plowshares and spears into pruning hooks and nation shall not lift up sword against nation anymore.

Then shall come to pass that city seen by John, a city yet to come, with gleaming towers and peaceful people. A city of justice and salaam. A city of kindness and shalom. A city "coming down out of heaven from God, prepared as a bride adorned for her husband." In that city, God will be with us. "And God will wipe every tear from our eyes. And death will be no more" (Rev 21:2–4).

Keep in your hearts the vision of a city like that and it will come! It will come!

Faith Triumphant

{≈≈≈}

Richard Land

*The Reverend Dr. Richard Land is president of The
Southern Baptist Convention's Ethics & Religious Liberty
Commission, in Nashville, Tennessee. He delivered this
sermon at Immanuel Baptist Church, Lebanon, Tennessee,
where he serves as interim pastor.*

I STRUGGLED THROUGH THE WEEK about what God
would have me say when I came in front of the sacred desk of the pulpit. God sent me first to 1 Peter.
The cross is the symbol of our faith. It is an empty
cross because our Savior has paid the price for our
sins. As the Great High Priest, he has entered once
into the place of sacrifice and it suffices. The cross
symbolizes the vertical aspect of our faith. We do not
reach up to God, it's God who reaches down and
makes connection with us in His Son, Jesus Christ.

So we must first look to the vertical aspect of our
faith. The Apostle Peter, a fisherman, says: "Be sub-
ject, one to another, and be clothed, with humility. For
God resisteth the proud, and giveth grace to the humble" (1 Pet. 5:5-6). We have been humbled this past
week, in the very best sense of that term. We have

been forced to come to a new understanding that our security cannot be in our economy. Our security cannot be in our material wealth. Our security cannot be ultimately in our military might. Our security is beyond ourselves. It must be found in God.

As a nation, we have reached for the deepest resources of our spiritual faith and of our history. During the great crisis times of our history, our presidents have called our nation to prayer and repentance, as President Bush did this past week.

We have found our strength and we have found our comfort on our knees before the Lord Jesus Christ and our Father. "God resisteth the proud, God giveth grace to the humble. Humble yourselves, therefore, under the mighty hand of God" (1 Pet. 5:5-6). Put yourselves under the mighty hand of God. He is sufficient. He is omniscient. He is all-powerful.

Then Peter uses the word that would be used for a Galilean fisherman flinging out or "casting" a net upon the water. He says, "Cast your cares on Him, for He careth for you" (v. 7). Cast your cares on Him. Give them to God.

I spoke with my parents, as many of you have done this week. My father was on a heavy cruiser about a hundred miles outside of Pearl Harbor when it was attacked. My mother had recently graduated from high school and entered the workforce. They described to me the enormous change that took place in our nation as we grasped the horror of Pearl Harbor. After December 7, 1941, there were no isolationists and internationalists. There were no Democrats and Republicans. There were just Americans.

Even with the grief that fills my heart, I have never felt better about my country and her future than I do at this moment. We are seeing what this nation is really made of. No one is complaining about children praying in school. No one is asking, "Is it appropriate for the president to say, 'Yes I pray every day, several times a day, in the Oval Office'?" No one is questioning the spiritual resources of our nation this morning.

We have indeed "Cast our cares on Him." And we have come with bent knee and humble spirit saying, "God, give us wisdom. God, give us strength."

We must always remember the rock from whence we are hewn and from where our strength will come (Isa. 51:1). And as we look at the vertical, now I want us to move to the horizontal aspect of our faith also symbolized in the cross.

Turn with me to Hebrews chapter 13. As we rest in Him and as we find our strength renewed, as we cast our cares on Him, as we humble ourselves before Him, the writer to the Hebrews says: "Let brotherly love continue. Be not forgetful to entertain strangers. Remember them that are in bonds as bound with them and them which suffer adversity, as being yourselves also in the body" (Heb. 13:1-3).

We are to reach out and to grieve with those that grieve and to remember those who are in suffering as though we suffer with them. We have seen an incredible, spontaneous outpouring of generosity and of courage. "Remember them that are in bonds, as bound with them." We need to pray for those who were injured. We need to pray for the families who lost loved ones. We need to pray for our countrymen. We need to pray for those brave men and women who serve in our nation's military.

I was reminded this week, as the announcement was made of the first fifty thousand troops to be called up, of when my own father was called to active duty. Our family was on vacation, and we heard on the radio that my father, who was in the Naval Reserves, had been called back to active duty by President Kennedy in the wake of the Berlin crisis. The ship he served on was being recalled to active duty. As a fifteen-year-old boy, I saw my father board a plane and fly to Key West, Florida, to get on a destroyer to prepare for antisubmarine warfare, to protect convoys crossing the Atlantic, and to reinforce Europe if the Russians tried to attack Berlin. At fifteen I was suddenly the "man of the house."

That scenario is about to be repeated all across this nation. We need to express our gratitude to our servicemen and our servicewomen. We need to express our gratitude to their families, and we need to do so in more than verbal ways as they cope with the loss of their loved ones' presence, as they go into harm's way to protect our freedom.

But there is another aspect of our horizontal faith. Turn to Matthew 5:38. Jesus commands us: "You have heard that it hath been said, 'An eye for an eye, and a tooth for a tooth,' but I say unto you, that ye resist not evil, but whosoever shall smite thee on thy right cheek, turn to him the other also. . . . Love your enemies, bless them that curse you, do good to them that hate you and pray for them which despitefully use you and persecute you, that you may be the children of your Father which is in Heaven" (Matt. 5:38-45).

Now this is hard. We do not have the right to hate these terrorists. God loved them. God sent Jesus to die for them. No matter how twisted, no matter how perverted by hate and vengeance they have become, we lower ourselves to their level if we harbor hatred and animosity in our hearts toward them as individuals.

In most cases, except for their leaders, they are victims. They are victims just as much as the generation of Hitler youth that was warped by Nazism and as much as those young Japanese pilots were poisoned by the leaders that taught them that they went instantly into heaven if they flew their planes into our ships.

We do not have the right to personal vengeance, but we do have the right to expect our government to exact justice. When Jesus talks about turning the other cheek, He is talking about us individually. If somebody kills my wife, I do not have the right to seek vengeance. But I do have a right to expect that the divinely ordained civil government will bring the perpetrators to justice to the fullest extent of the law.

The Apostle Paul made it clear that God ordained government for that very reason: "The powers that be are ordained of God. For he is the minister of God to thee for good. But if thou do that which is evil, be afraid; for he beareth not the sword in vain: for he is the minister of God, a revenger to execute wrath upon him that doeth evil" (Rom. 13:1-4).

We have a right to expect the government to exact justice on the perpetrators of these crimes, and our enemy is not Islam. These people are no more legitimate followers of Islam than the Marxist murderers who call themselves Catholics in the IRA are legitimate adherents of that faith.

We had an eerily similar episode in our history. In 1800, Thomas Jefferson was elected president in a very controversial election that went into the House of Representatives. In the very first months of his presidency, Thomas Jefferson was confronted by the Barbary states of North Africa, who were harboring pirates who went out as terrorists and captured ships and held their crews, cargo, and passengers for ransom. America had been paying tribute to keep the pirates from attacking our ships. When the pirates tried to raise the ante, Jefferson, who was repulsed by the tribute to begin with, said, "Never."

America, still a young nation, sent a fleet to the Mediterranean. The Marine Corps hymn begins, "From the halls of Montezuma, to the shores of Tripoli." Tripoli was where they defeated the pirate terrorists. America took care of the problem at its source. Now it is time to do it again.

What about you? What if you were a passenger on one of the hijacked planes? What if you were one of those people trapped in the buildings targeted by these terrorists?

We never know when we are going to meet eternity. We never know when we are going to be faced with our mortality. Are you ready? Do you know of your future beyond this life? You can. Jesus died to make it possible for you to know. He died on the cross in our place, and the Bible says: "These are written that ye might believe that Jesus is the Christ, the Son of God, and that believing ye might have life through his name" (John 20:31).

It appears that at least two classmates of mine perished on the upper floors of the World Trade Center. If I had been there, I know that the minute my life was extinguished, I would be in the presence of Jesus forever and ever. Not because of my morality, not because of my good deeds, but because I placed my life and destiny in the arms of Jesus Christ when I trusted Him as Savior and Lord. I'm trusting Him and Him only for salvation, and He has promised that "he which hath begun a good work in you will perform it until the day of Jesus Christ" (Phil. 1:6).

And you can know that too, if you will trust Jesus as your savior.

The Human Heart and the Spirit of God

Jon P. Gunnemann

Dr. Jon P. Gunnemann, who teaches at Candler School of Theology at Emory University in Atlanta, Georgia, preached this sermon in Cannon Chapel on Thursday, September 13. It was published two weeks later in the Christian Century *magazine, from which the following is excerpted.*

OUR RESPONSE TO HUMAN HORROR and tragedy moves inexorably outward as if through concentric circles, beginning in the gut and the heart, moving to the head, and finally taking shape in the form of shared social responses. Planes exploding into buildings, bodies falling from the top floors, people running and screaming before an avalanche of debris, dust, and smoke: There is first a symbiosis of suspended belief and identifying empathy, a "this isn't happening" reaction combined with a sense of the terror and chaos experienced by the victims, an unreflective knowledge that this could be me, it could be you. Onlookers turning away, covering their eyes: That's the gut response of tears and churning nausea, of too much to bear.

Then there is a movement of sympathy and imagination, a bit of distance that's no less terrifying: What if one of the victims is someone you know and love? A friend or a member of your family? That's the heart, aided by the head, aching with pain and anxiety, driving us to telephones, to a desperate search for reassurance. And then the head tries to take control in an attempt to understand what is actually happening: Where, when, who, how? we ask. But finally the heart and the head come together in the question Why? And when we try to answer this question, we move toward the outer ring of the social imagination that orders our common lives.

We want to name the horror, give it meaning, domesticate it in the narrative of our lives. The search for meaning has been underway for days now, by the media, by government officials, by people on the street, all groping to recast a horror that rained from the skies into something we can understand. There are the adjectives and adverbs: outrage, infamy, cowardly terrorism; the metaphors: an attack on freedom, an attack on democracy, an act of war, an apocalyptic event. We search for historical allusions: Pearl Harbor has topped the list—the only other attack on American soil—but one New Yorker with a larger heart added Hiroshima. And finally, there is blame and the promise of retribution, the naming of the cause as evil with the solemn promise to punish it.

The president of the United States has now given official sanction to some of these interpretive framings: The attack was an "act of war"—that's necessary official language, connecting his responsibilities to the social meanings of the U.S. Constitution and the NATO treaty. We have seen a new kind of enemy who is dangerous and works from the shadows—that is a metaphorical and reasonably accurate interpretation of new forms of threat to national security both in the United States and elsewhere, inviting perhaps a rethinking of what security means in the modern world. We are engaged in a "monumental struggle between good and evil" and make no mistake about it, "good will win." That is cosmology, and comes close to a neat reversal and mimicry of the demonizing mentality that flew those planes into the World Trade Center and the Pentagon.

As Christians and as those called to be theologians for the church, we have other language and texts to command our loyalty, to shape our interpretations, to resist demonization, and to form the impulses of our hearts. Some of these we know well enough to recite from memory: Love your enemies, Do good to those who persecute you, Obey the ruling authorities, for they are ordained by God. But some are less well known and less comforting to the heart in pain.

Such is the lectionary text for September 16 from Jeremiah (4:11-12, 22-28), with unsettling historical parallels to our circumstances and a deeply disturbing interpretation of them. Judah has been conquered,

Jeremiah is in exile, and the aggressor is Babylon, pagans from the East, hostile to Jewish religion and practice, threatening Judah's religious and civic culture. Prescient foreshadowings of Saddam Hussein and Osama bin-Laden? But does Jeremiah blame Babylon, calling it evil? On the contrary, he blames Judah's lack of faithfulness to the covenant with Moses, its turn toward a religion based on royalty, its foolishness and stupidity! And he calls for Judah's repentance.

He does more: Babylon's aggression is portrayed as a hot wind that will blow across Judah, rendering fruitful land barren and laying waste to cities. And then Jeremiah employs his interpretive art, drawing unmistakably on the language of Genesis where the creative spirit gives form and life to the void and the chaos that existed prior to Creation. But this same creative spirit is now a destructive wind. Babylon's aggression is the wind of God, original creative Spirit now in judgment, reducing Judah to rubble and the chaos of pre-Creation because of its unfaithfulness.

Do we dare use this text for our circumstances? The roar of the wind of jets putting cities to ruin, laying waste fields in Pennsylvania—dare we call this the angry spirit of God? It's bad exegesis, isn't it, the way televangelists use biblical texts? Isn't it distressingly close to Saddam Hussein's interpretation of the events ("America is reaping the thorns it has sown")? Doesn't it imply a callous disregard for the deaths and suffering of innocents? And surely it is sacrilegious to suggest that God in some way willed this as punishment, a haunting echo of Nietzsche's not entirely mocking aphorism that the same power that can create can also destroy.

No, we cannot use the text this way, but we also cannot put it aside. Let us concede that Jeremiah was more confident in his reading of God's acts in history than we are, or at least than I am. Let us keep clearly in front of our eyes that to call the tragic events in New York and Washington the judgment or will of God commits us to similar judgments about all human misfortune, personal and collective, trivializing human suffering and rendering God capricious. But while keeping these points in clear focus, let us not miss the prophetic point of Jeremiah: That in the entanglements of human history and conflict, God's creative spirit and will transcend immediate human purposes and perceptions; that almost all human conflict is born out of a history of interactions, which on close inspection calls for repentance on all sides; and that in every conflict our hearts and imaginations become ironically connected to the hearts of the real and perceived enemy.

If we listen to Jeremiah this way, we may at least find our hearts reformed through meditation on some disturbing and sobering questions. Here is one line of questioning for meditation: The attack on two major cities, destroying the twin-spired symbol of American financial power and striking at the center of our military power, laid bare our vulnerability. That a score of men, armed only with knives, could do this tells us that it can be done again. There is an array of alternative weapons, many far more devastating and just as easy to wield. Is it possible that we have placed too much confidence in our technological, economic, and military power, imagining that they could render us invulnerable? Has our proud way of life, with its affluence and waste, given us the illusion of having conquered nature and the vicissitudes of life? Is it possible that we can discover through this event our common lot with the whole of humanity, for the vast majority of whom everyday life is precarious? Might we be led to question American exceptionalism? Might we be willing to cast our lot with the whole of humanity and the whole of God's creation? Might our hearts be shaped in such a way that, whatever we do, we come to understand that our destiny is intimately bound up with the destiny of the whole of creation, and with the limits placed on that creation by the wind of God, God's breath of life?

Another line of questions for our further meditation: How is it that groups of people, created in the image of God, hate the United States so much that they could carry out these horrendous acts of violence? Yes, we can give psychological answers, interpretations of the hearts and heads of others. Maybe some insights can be found, but psychologizing is always tricky stuff.

Or we might look for religious answers, pointing to passages in the scriptures of others, but there we will find at best ambiguities equally present in our own scriptures. But what if we trace the conflicts and divisions of the Middle East through their historical entanglements? On one side we would have to trace the almost endless conflicts between Arabs and Jews in the last half century; and behind that the founding of the state of Israel with British and European support, with Zionism revived; and behind that the Holocaust in the first half of the last century, with Jews fleeing Christian Europe; and before that we would find the Christian progroms against the Jews, and the Crusades against the Muslims in the Middle Ages; and earlier the persecution by Imperial Rome of Christians; and still earlier the wars recorded in the Old Testament—Joshua laying waste to Jericho. And through the debris and horror of these historical, mutual entanglements, we might come to see, first dimly in the dust, the power of religion, and then perhaps more clearly understand with a sober balance of horror and humility the capacity of human beings to do great evil under banners of good.

Hard questions, these, with no easy answers. But the very asking of them might at least save us from becoming like those who have injured us, and might lead us to genuine acts of repentance. Asking them might create a proper humility in the interpretation of September 11, even while we genuinely grieve, and it might help in discovering proportionate ways to respond in achieving the genuine security we need. The impulses of the heart are shaped by the interpretations we give and find, and the narrative for which we are willing to settle reveals where the heart finally is, and how we will act. Might we come back from the imaginative circle of Jeremiah's interpretation with cleansed and renewed hearts?

The events of September 11 will always resist our attempts at interpretation because their magnitude represents an intersecting of innumerable histories unique to each person involved—victim, mourner, defender, fireman, nurse, onlooker, government official, and yes, even perpetrator's complexity of intersecting histories that no single interpretation can comprehend. And beyond these unique histories and perspectives lies the commonality of our historical entanglements. Interpret we must, but any interpretation can yield at most a partial truth, never a complete truth. And great human tragedy cuts too deeply into our personal and collective consciousness, well below the articulating capacities of our conscious minds, no matter how creative we may be.

Billy Collins, our national poet laureate, spoke of the helplessness of poetry in the face of these events: "At a time like this, it is best to read a Psalm." Perhaps we should at this time do only that, standing in solidarity with more than two millennia of Jews and Christians who have turned to the Psalms at times of personal and communal agony, when the question

Why? defies answer, and we find ourselves able only to express the pain and suffering in our hearts while at the same time singing praise to the maker of heaven and earth, the wind of life, the author of our being. That too shapes the impulses of the heart.

Who's in Charge Here?

Paul Gonyea

The Reverend Paul Gonyea is minister of the Atlanta Church of Religious Science. In addition to fulfilling the requirements of a large spiritual community, he has been a professional pilot for twenty-eight years, including twenty-two years with a major airline. At present, the Reverend Gonyea flies weekly trips to Europe.

WHAT A DIFFERENCE A WEEK MAKES. Last week we were dressed in Hawaiian shirts, getting ready for our annual picnic. Today, we're in mourning.

This was a very difficult talk for me to prepare. Not because there isn't much to say, but because there is so much to say. I've been listening to so many words for the last five days, and so have you, from people far more eloquent than I am, and part of me feels there isn't anything else to say. I can't tell you how many times this week I just wanted to sit down in a corner and cry.

As a minister and teacher, I deal in words. But there are no words to describe the indescribable. We've all been looking at the television images, over and over and over again, and they still don't seem real. Part of us keeps waiting for Bruce Willis or Arnold Schwarzenegger to show up in a helicopter and save the day. But they don't show up. Or we keep waiting for an advertisement to come on the television and tell us that what we're seeing is actually a promotion for some blockbuster, high-budget disaster movie coming out next month. But it's not.

I was thinking the other day: If the events of this week had actually been advertised months ago as a movie instead of being a real-life nightmare, millions of people would have rushed to see it as soon as it opened. In fact, people all over the world would shell out millions of dollars to see it. And the sad truth is — as a movie — we would have found it entertaining. That alone should tell us that the problem we face as a race of human beings is something more than just a security breakdown, something more than just a terrorist threat. The greatest problem we face right now is not in the world; it is in our collective consciousness. And if we don't come up with a spiritual solution very soon — in addition to any political solution we might come up with — and figure out how to implement it, then I'm afraid we've seen only the opening round of a very long, sad chain of events.

What happened on Tuesday was a tragic, heartbreaking, unthinkable disaster, completely beyond anything we could imagine. Some of you may have lost friends and family. Some of you probably lost people you worked with. And in a way, we all lost our innocence. The problems of the world we've been reading about on a daily basis "over there" are now "over here."

When we woke up on Wednesday morning, we all believed that the world had completely changed. But the truth is, it hadn't changed much at all. It was moving in the same direction it's been moving for years. The only difference was, it had finally reached a point that affected us personally—it finally reached a level that caught our attention.

We (and by *we* I mean every person and every country in the world) have been creating this society we are living in for quite some time now. As big a shock as this was, it did *not* come out of nowhere; it came as a direct result of things we have done and things we have not done. It came out of beliefs we have accepted without question, and beliefs we have refused to acknowledge. It came out of those things we have focused on, and those things we have refused to look at. The only real difference between last week and this week is that now we can see that our world is larger than we thought. And we now see that we can no longer separate ourselves from it; not physically (borders mean nothing now), not emotionally—and especially not spiritually.

But what do we do? That's the hard part. We all know there are many important decisions we're going to have to make very soon—as individuals, as Americans, and as members of the human race. And the scary thing about it is, the kind of world we create for ourselves and for those who live after us will depend upon the wisdom—or the insanity—of the decisions we make. As we find ourselves immersed in this present wave of extreme emotion—as these graphic pictures and stories of death and destruction are poured into us from every television, every newsstand, every conversation—it is especially important that we stay in close touch with the Divine Truth of our being. Because, as spiritual beings, the best that we are shines through *only* when we express emotions that support the ideas of Life, Love, and Peace. That means in every situation, no matter *how* difficult that situation may be.

Most of the world has been accomplishing this over the last few days through prayer; that's good. In our teaching, prayer is simply the conscious recognition of a Higher Truth, a Higher Power, which is everywhere present. I think Emerson said it best when he wrote that "Prayer is the contemplation of the facts of life from a higher point of view."

But that means, if it is to be effective, prayer has to be in harmony with the best of Life, in harmony with a loving and intelligent creative power. It works, for example, only as long as we are praying for peace instead of victory; as long as we are praying for an end to *all* suffering, everywhere, not just in our own country. It works as long as we aren't praying for God to help us destroy another human being or another country.

If we believe that God is on our side instead of theirs, we are making the same mistake as the people who carried out this attack. Because God isn't on anybody's side; as a matter of fact, we're all supposed to be on God's side.

As we deal with the immediate aftereffects of what has happened, it's important that we *all* look at what is in our hearts and on our minds as we prepare to take the next step. Because we are in charge of something very important. We are in charge of what happens in our world from here on out. We alone are in charge of what we allow to stay and grow in our consciousness. The danger is, there are many other people and ideologies and emotions competing for our attention. And if we choose to give them our attention—consciously or unconsciously—if we somehow give in to the ideas that they are pushing on us, we won't be in charge anymore. And that concerns me.

Let me start with the hard stuff. Let's start with how we are thinking, with our beliefs, about the people who carried out this attack. We're going to have to face this eventually. How do we reconcile the concepts of vengeance and retaliation and justice (by God!) with forgiveness and understanding and love for all people? It may seem almost impossible to forgive anyone who did something so horrible, but that is exactly why it is important that we do so. Not for their sake, but for ours.

Let's face it: Either these spiritual truths we claim

to believe work all the time, or they don't work at all. When Jesus said, "Forgive your enemies," *these* are the kind of people he was talking about, not just some guy who cut you off in traffic. The Buddha said, "We must see God in every person." We have to ask ourselves: What is truly in our consciousness when we think about these people and what they did? If you can answer that question honestly for yourself, you'll have a much better understanding of your own level of spiritual growth.

I have a personal interest at stake here that some of you may not know about. I grew up in a military family, attended the Air Force Academy, and flew military aircraft in Southeast Asia. I have never been accused of being a bleeding heart liberal. I've spent twenty-two years in the cockpit of large commercial airliners. In fact, for the last few years, I have been flying the same kind of aircraft taken by the hijackers. I know what the cockpit looks like, up close and personal. I have flown those same routes, taken off and landed many times at those same airports, and carried thousands of passengers, people like you and me, just going on vacation or on a business trip. When I think of what happened in those airplanes, I have trouble breathing. I can identify completely with those pilots; I know their last thoughts were of complete personal failure, helplessness, and despair. That's what I would have felt.

But if I allow myself to be consumed with the rage that I feel tugging at the edge of my psyche, then those madmen who did this will have won. They will have taken from me my power to choose how I look at Life, to choose what I believe about the goodness of Life, and—in the process—they will have enlisted me in accelerating this cycle of violence.

As long as we choose to remain grounded in our spiritual center—and it is our choice—as long as we hold fast to our belief that love is always stronger than fear, knowing that this is the only possible way we are ever going to find a solution over the long run, everything they accomplished will be in vain. Instead of creating the fear they tried to create, they will have created a common bond, a spiritual bond, not just between Americans, but between all people, everywhere, who recognize the power of love as the only real power in the world. And that just might push us to another level in our spiritual evolution.

Do the people who planned this need to be stopped? Of course they do. Do they need to be brought to justice and held accountable, do we need to demonstrate to everyone, everywhere, that this behavior is unacceptable in a civilized society? Yes, we need to do that too. But *how* we do this is not nearly as important as the consciousness with which we do it. We have every right to be angry, but we have to be very careful about where we allow that anger to take us.

A man on the radio a few days ago said something I thought was very profound; he said it's important to save Americans, but it's also important that we save

America, that we protect the ideals that make this country such a powerful source of good in the world. Sure we make mistakes. And sure, saving human lives is important. But this country was founded on certain universal spiritual ideals that give human life much of its meaning. "What does it matter if we gain the world, if in the process we lose our soul" (Mark 8:36).

This is not a battle between good and evil, or a battle between the forces of light and darkness. There are no battles being fought within the Mind of God. Satan was not guiding those aircraft, as I heard some American religious fanatic say the other day. They were hijacked and destroyed by angry, extremist, intolerant fanatics, who never learned that there's only one God, and we're all One with It. We have to be careful not to get locked into an *us* versus *them* mentality. We're all *us*. And we're all *them*.

This is not about winning a battle, it is about revealing a Truth. It is about, first and foremost, our ability to become aware—to reveal the Truth to ourselves—that we are all spiritual beings, that we are all perfect ideas in the mind of a loving, peaceful God. And then it is about letting that awareness be revealed in every corner of the world. Whatever it takes to make that happen, that's what we need to do.

The only hope we can have for what happened this week is to heal it at the heart level, at the soul level. Deepak Chopra wrote in a letter this week that this is a deep wound on the heart of humanity. And it affects us all. It has to. This was an attack on all of civilization, but it did not just come from "out there"; we have to recognize the contribution of what is "in here." If this is an attack on all of us, then all of us have played a part in creating a world where this can happen. And all of us need to work together to figure out how we can heal a collective consciousness that can create something so unimaginable.

This isn't about who we blame; it's about how we heal. And the place we need to start is in our own heart. Why? Because, if it doesn't happen there, it isn't likely to happen anywhere. This is the Truth in your life. And this is the Truth in mine.

A New Christianity for a New World

John Shelby Spong

The Right Reverend John Shelby Spong, eighth bishop of Newark, was the guest preacher at Harvard Memorial Church, in Cambridge, Massachusetts, on September 16. Adapting the thesis of his new book by the same title (published by HarperCollins), he pointed to the tragedy of five days before to question our understanding of God.

S INCE LAST TUESDAY images of airplanes, loaded with both human beings and gasoline, crashing into the World Trade Center have been etched eternally on our consciousness. The faces of terrorism have become indelible. The willingness on the part of fanatics to die for beliefs deeply held is at one and the same time disturbing, powerful, and almost unbelievable. The randomness of death has become vivid. Chance has come to be recognized as a major part of reality. Stories are already circulating about people who were scheduled to be on one of those flights but who changed their plans for some reason or about meetings that had been planned for the World Trade

Center on that particular day that had been canceled. Those stories cry out for a divine purpose, for some meaning other than coincidence, and yet no explanation makes sense.

If God was or is really in charge, how did this tragedy occur? It is not a new question. It is asked every time a hurricane strikes or an earthquake erupts. It was asked by the Jewish people in the wake of the Holocaust. It is a question designed to keep us from despairing over the fact that there is a deep suspicion, seldom spoken by human lips, that we just might be alone in this vast, chaotic, and frequently painful world. The theistic God, that supernatural parent figure who lives beyond the sky, and who has the power to intervene in order to protect us, may well be our own creation, designed to speak to that anxiety. When tragedies occur and divine protection is not forthcoming, the heart faces the hysteria of our self-conscious humanity and we struggle to restore our supernatural theistic God to believability.

The issue posed by Archibald MacLeish more than a generation ago in a play based on the Book of Job, is still poignant. "If God is God, God is not good. If God is good, God is not God." That is, if God has the power to prevent tragedy and yet does not use it, then God is malevolent and immoral, not good at all. If God, on the other hand, does not have the power to prevent tragedy, then God is impotent.

Is atheism then our only alternative? Must we

human beings simply gird our loins about us, put on stoical, existential faces and stare our cold godless reality down, while we get about the task of living courageously in a meaningless world? Or can we use a moment like this current crisis, as devastating and anxiety producing as it has been, to consider anew our very understanding of God, or at least to seek new God definitions to fit a new world?

In the childhood of our humanity, when believing was easy, we thought that the planet earth was the center of the universe, basking in a supernatural God's constant attentiveness. The biblical story reflects this confidence and that worldview. We believed that a theistic God directed the affairs of human history from the divine perch above the sky. This God, we were convinced, controlled the weather, sending the great flood on Noah, and periodic droughts with their resulting famines on Israel. This God could even demonstrate the ability to still the storm in the life of Jesus. This God kept record books on us all, punishing us with sickness or forgiving us with healing. This God blessed our nation with victory and fought our enemies for us. This was the God who blasted the Egyptians with plague after plague, who split the Red Sea to allow the chosen ones to escape and who then closed that sea to allow the enemies of the chosen ones to drown. We were confident in those days that human life was at the very center of all that is. Then came that frightening day when the centrality of the earth was supplanted, first by the sun in the groundbreaking insights of Copernicus and Galileo and later through the work of the astrophysicists in their recognition that the universe actually has no center, since it is still expanding.

Today we live with the knowledge that this tiny planet earth rotates around a middle class star in a galaxy called the Milky Way that contains, in addition to our sun, over 100 billion other stars. Yet our single galaxy is so large that it takes light, traveling at the approximate speed of 186,000 miles per second, more than 100,000 years to go from one end of our galaxy to the other. The mind boggles just trying to imagine that! We also live with the knowledge that our galaxy is only one of more than 125 billion other galaxies in the visible universe. A supernatural God who might direct the affairs of human history from some vantage point above the sky is quite frankly no longer believable. We try to ignore that reality out of an abiding anxiety, but then a human tragedy forces that realization anew into our consciousness; it raises questions that are unavoidable.

Is a supernatural, miracle-working, invasive deity the only way to think of God? That becomes the burning theological issue essential to address so that we can endure the traumas that living always seems to thrust upon us.

To seek an answer, consider the minority voices in our sacred writings. Among the people of the world, there are always those who do not swim in the majority ponds. They are the people who are willing to probe new arenas, to look at meaning in different ways. They do not confuse their God experiences with the familiar God explanations of their times. Those minority voices, always present in the hidden recesses of our sacred story, might aid our quest for a new God concept, perhaps a new God metaphor, or even a new pathway into the presence of the Holy.

The Jewish people throughout their history seemed to know that God and the popular definition of God could never be identical. That is why they spoke so vehemently against idolatry, against trying to capture God in any human image. That is why the name of God could never be spoken. They instinctively knew that nothing could finally capture the Holy. Not words, not scriptures, not creeds, not human theological constructs. Nothing can capture the reality of God.

So despite the fact that in the scriptures, while the popular mind spoke of the supernatural God who did miracles, the minority report in the biblical story saw God after the analogy of a series of impersonal images. This minority voice spoke of God, for example, as the wind. The wind was formless, mysterious. They did not know from whence the wind came or where it went. It was incapable of being defined or placed within boundaries. One could only experience the wind. One could not define it. The purpose of the wind was simply to animate, to vitalize, to give life. This image of God as wind is seen in the Creation story where God creates Adam out of the dust of the earth like a child making a mud pie. But Adam is lifeless and inert. Then God is portrayed as giving Adam mouth-to-mouth resuscitation, filling him with God's breath, thought by this era to be the source of the wind. Only then did Adam come to life. Life itself, says this biblical insight, is the medium through which the Holy lives. God is not a being sitting on a cloud somewhere. God is the dynamic, emerging source of life.

The Bible also defines God with the word "love." God is love says the Epistle of John and whoever abides in love abides in God! Love, the Bible suggests, comes to consciousness in the human experience. Love makes life possible. It is love that creates wholeness. Whenever love is shared, life is enhanced. Whenever hatred replaces love, life is diminished. So the minority voice of the Bible says that God is love. I suggest that an even keener insight emerges when we reverse those words. For if God is love, then love is God. Please hear that biblical insight: Love is what God is. If you want to make God visible you do so, not by having a vision, or by receiving a revelation from on high, but by loving—loving wastefully.

It is this God that I confront when the theistic God images of the past crumble and fall apart amid the irrationalities of life with its violence and pain. Neither you nor I can control our fate in this world. Reality does not provide us with that option. We cannot make secure our fragile lives. What we can do, however, is to commit ourselves in every moment to live fully, to love wastefully, and to be all that we can be. That is the way, perhaps the only way, that the world that is being born in our day will experience the reality of God. That is the way we will touch transcendence and thus enter the deepest mystery of both life and God.

The worship of this God is not a magic potion. It will not keep us safe, but it will drive us into a new humanity that is now beyond our limits. It will dispel the need that is within us to find acts of revenge that only expand the cycle of violence. Beyond all else this worship will enable us to discover God within ourselves in a way that is profoundly new. A commitment will emerge, together with a sense of responsibility that becomes almost a calling, to live our lives in such a way as to build a new world in which all people will have a better chance to experience God by living fully, loving wastefully, and being all that they are capable of being in the infinite variety of the human family. A new mission for a new church will have been born. Human beings will have become cocreators with God of a new world.

Lost Sheep, Lost Coins

Brenda G. Husson

*Rector of Saint James Episcopal Church in Manhattan, the
Reverend Brenda G. Husson preached on Luke 15:1-10,
Jesus' parable of the lost coin.*

A S THE DAYS GO BY, many of us feel more confused, not less. As the first shock wears off,
some of the protective numbness slips away as well.
We are all aware now that the pain may well get worse
before it gets better and that the days of smoke and
dust and digging will not go on for days, but for weeks.

We have had our comforts and our miracles—the
calls I know most of us have received from friends we
lost touch with years ago checking to make sure we
were all right. E-mails have been arriving at the parish
all week, some from the friends of this parish in northern Ireland and southern Africa sending us love and
prayers that come not only from the heart but from
hearts that have known their own terror and pain and
grief. Even the pictures of vast crowds around this

country and around the world holding candles, keeping silence, murmuring prayers help. Nothing helps more than the stories of the people who are alive when we feared we would never see them again. The stories of alarm clocks that didn't work or trains missed that made people wonderfully late to work, and the stories of people — some in this room — who made it down unimaginable flights of stairs in time to head north and head home.

But it isn't all miracles. The missing are not just pictures posted all over this city, though those pictures keep us in tears. The missing and dead are our friends. The missing and dead are our own parishioners. The missing and dead are our neighbors, including firefighters from the fire station that guards our church. And even those who made it down the stairs or back across the plaza or out of the neighborhood know that getting out is a long way from getting back to normal.

There are two reasons, at least, why our grief does not settle, two reasons, at least, why we will be in tears for a long time to come. They are good reasons and even godly ones. The first is that we have discovered, or been reminded, through this unspeakable act of terrorism, that there is nothing that separates us from each other. John Guare wrote a wonderful play some years back called *Six Degrees of Separation*, suggesting there were never more than six people separating any of us from any other person on the planet. I thought he was right. But he wasn't. It turns out there's no separation at all. The pictures of the missing include everyone. The very poor struggling to support families on almost nothing and the heads of companies that manage billions. They are there in three-piece suits and janitors' uniforms, immigrants and lifelong New Yorkers. And they look just right next to each other on those walls. The clothes or the color or the background just doesn't matter. Because they are all of them someone that somebody loves. We haven't just known that in our heads this week, we've known it in our guts and our hearts and our souls. That love breaks down the dividing walls between us and connects us all. If our hearts break, how dare we who are made in God's own image, think that God's does not? For God made each of them. God knows them all as his children. God calls each one by name.

Realizing that, we have been our best selves this week. Looking out for each other. Doing it with great gentleness and often in tears. The second good and godly reason we find ourselves still weeping is that we have learned or relearned what matters. Terror sought to strike at the heart of our country—at two twinned towers that stood as monuments to financial power and a culture of consumption. They stood for that, no question. But as rubble they have come to stand for a much more noble and more lasting truth. That what matters most is love. That is what lasts and that was being raised up even in the awful moments when those towers came down.

Nothing separates us from each other, and love matters most. We forget that when life seems normal. God never does. We forget that when we believe we are in charge. God never does. We forget that when our days go on uninterrupted. God *never* does.

I have always found it hard to preach about the lost coin. It always seems so trivial since it's just a coin like nine others and worth very little in the marketplace. It makes more sense these days, when family members may be identified by a small scar or a scrap of a wallet. If a coin were the sign of connection we know now we would search for it for weeks. Some will not find so much as that. Yet the parables are not really about a woman searching her house or a shepherd scouring a hillside. The parables are about God. And about us. About a God who searches as if we are the greatest treasure there is. About a God who searches as if we are the most precious sheep in the flock. Because we are. We all of us are. We do not forget the people we love just because they are one among thousands. How could we think for a minute that God does? God does not forget. Does not forget to love us. Does not forget to search for us. Does not forget to find us. And having found us, God does not let us go. Not in life. Not in death. Not ever. That is the Gospel promise. We are all lost. But we are all loved. We shall all be found. And we shall all be raised up at the last day.

This week, in one of the several services that took place in this city, a rabbi and an imam stood and embraced behind a Christian pulpit. They said to the gathered congregation, "We are your prayer." They were right, but not entirely so. For no one person, or even two, can be the prayer for us all. But all of us together can be God's prayer. All of us can bear God's image into the world. All of us must if the world is to learn the truths we have found in this tragedy.

So I ask you now to take the hand of the person sitting next to you. Please close your eyes and remember in silence all those who have been lost in this week's tragedy. . . . The people we remember are like that lost sheep or that missing coin. They have been found. They are treasured. They are home.

The person whose hand you hold is also a lost sheep, a missing coin. The person whose hand you hold is searched for and treasured and will be brought home to great rejoicing. We become God's prayer and show forth God's image when we hold onto the people we know. When we hold onto the people we don't. When we hold on even to our enemies. God holds us all that we might all know his saving embrace. Let us be God's prayer. Let us be God's image. This week and in all the weeks to come until we are *all* finally home with God.

The Tears of Pain,
Tears of Promise

C. Welton Gaddy

*The Reverend Dr. C. Welton Gaddy is executive director of
the Interfaith Alliance headquartered in Washington D.C.
A Baptist minister and ecumenical activist, he preached this
sermon at Northminster Church in Monroe, Louisiana,
where he serves as minister of preaching and worship.*

IN THE FACE OF TERROR, violence, and hurt, Jewish minds often turned to a place called Ramah and Jewish voices spoke of a woman named Rachel weeping for her children. Perhaps you recall Rachel, the younger daughter of Laban, the second wife of Jacob, and the mother of Joseph and Benjamin. In the years after her death, people spoke of Rachel as the mother of the Northern Kingdom — Israel — people who were ripped from their homeland, taken captive, and made to live as exiles in a foreign land, the "children" for whom Rachel wept.

The author of the Gospel called "Matthew" thought of Rachel as he wrote about the slaughter of innocent babies mandated by a paranoid king. When King Herod received news of the birth of a child named Jesus, a baby whom some spoke of as a king, Herod, worried about a rival to his throne, ordered the execution of male infants throughout the region of Bethlehem. Disturbed by this narrative that was a part of the story of Jesus' birth, Matthew's thoughts raced to Rachel. The Gospel writer incorporated into his narrative a piece of prophetic poetry about Rachel drawn from the oracles of the eighth-century Jeremiah.

> *A voice was heard in Ramah,*
> *wailing and loud lamentation,*
> *Rachel was weeping for her children;*
> *she refused to be consoled,*
> *because they were no more.* (Jer. 31:15)

I have always been deeply moved by the depth of the pathos in this Hebrew verse. Note the emphasis on Rachel's refusal to have her grief consoled by arguments born of rationalization. I identify with Rachel and respect her resistance to insipid logic that would be best replaced by silence. No doubt, you are well acquainted with argumentative statements of comfort. "Remember that others also have sorrows," someone says to a hurting woman (a fact that, if really heard by the woman in grief, only doubles her pain). Then there is always the familiar assertion, "It could have been worse, you know" (another observation inept at diminishing hurt).

An always-look-on-the-bright-side person says to a weeper, "Don't forget that this terrible trauma can make us stronger" (a possibility perhaps, but not one that alters in any way the hurt deep in the heart of the one in grief). Seldom, if ever, is logic the parent of comfort in the face of grinding grief. Rachel, bless her, would have none of the glib relief offered by her peers. Rachel's children were gone, no more, and she refused to be consoled.

Through the long, heavy hours of the past tragedy-filled days, over and over again my mind has gone to the biblical words about Rachel weeping for her children. In a sense this Hebrew woman was, and is, the voice of the world's weeping. Sometime between the early morning hours of last Tuesday and this moment of divine worship today, if not before that time, we became members of Rachel's family. This morning she is our sister.

Tears appear in our eyes, but they come from our hearts fed by thoughts in our minds and feelings that dominate our emotions. During the last several days, weeping has covered our land like the heavy dew of an oppressively humid summer morning or like the first killing frost on the leaves of trees in autumn. Rachel is weeping for her children.

Why? Why do we weep? What is the substance of our pain? Many have lost the loves of their lives and others the lives of their lovers. The personal dimension of the nation's hurt is inestimable in scope. Gone too for even more people is a taken-for-granted sense of security that has been replaced by a pervasive, unnerving awareness of vulnerability. We now know all too well that deadly blasts like those we once associated only with places like Kosovo, Chechnya, or Nairobi are realities in the places where we play, love, pray, and work. No longer can citizens of this land dream the national dream apart from the possibility of an occasional nightmare.

Rachel is our sister. We are weeping.

We best pay attention to our tears. Frederick Buechner says that our tears, especially the unexpected ones, tell us something about the secret of who we are. According to Buechner, God speaks to us through our tears; God speaks to us about the mystery of where we have come from and summons us to where, if we are to be safe, we should go next. We best pay attention to our tears.

In recent hours, I have wept over what has happened. I have listened to friends in New York describe the devastation that has touched one family after another indiscriminately. I have spoken with numerous leaders in the tradition of Islam and shared the pain they feel as a result of gross stereotyping and senseless harassment even as they met to pray for our nation. I have talked extensively with people in Washington almost disoriented by military police on the streets, F-16's overhead, hovering smoke, and one screaming siren after another. I have wept over what has happened. Honestly, though, my gravest concerns and bitterest tears are prompted by thoughts of the future rather than by reflections on the past. How we react to what has happened will shape our nation even more profoundly than the terrorists' attacks on our citizens and national institutions.

Let me tell you about my tears and the sources from which they flow. As do you, I know well my sister Rachel.

I weep in the presence of a preoccupation with and an exaltation of violence. The terrorists who assaulted our nation must not be allowed to draw us into an international contest in which chauvinism is deemed more important than reason, firepower is considered superior to moral influence, and might is equated with right.

Please understand that I appreciate and support the necessity of our government providing for the public welfare and protecting national security. I praise President Bush for the patience to which he has pledged himself and his administration in pursuing appropriate responses to the horrific acts fomented upon our nation this past week. I applaud those members of Congress who have called for an intensive search for alternatives of response that do not all magnify violence. I trust civil strategists far wiser than me in the ways to advance and accomplish our national goals. But, I weep when I hear shouts of encouragement for indiscriminate campaigns of violence, which, if carried out, will leave us with no differentiation in character from the fear-mongers of the world and will rob us of international influence independent of power.

Rachel is weeping for her children; and she is not alone.

I weep in the presence of raw hatred. Among the many disturbing images that have taken up residence in our psyches during the past several days, one picture in particular haunts me like no other. I see a young Palestinian boy who lives somewhere in the war-riddled, occupied territory of Israel. It's Tuesday of last week. The young lad is grinning from ear to ear, jumping up and down, and cheering as he hears the news of our nation's hurt. Obviously this youngster, barely a teenager if he is that old, has no thoughts for the people who died in the cities of New York and Washington, D.C., or on a piece of rural terrain outside Pittsburgh, Pennsylvania. This little boy is not thinking that someone like him lost a father or a mother (though maybe he already has lost both his father and mother in the violence of the Middle East). He seems insensitive to the assault on stability that ultimately will reach into the presently besieged village where he lives and negatively impact the future that he faces. This young boy was cheering hurt in the United States because of hatred that someone taught him.

No child is born with hatred in his or her heart. Hatred is learned behavior, the result of expert teachers who both speak and model bitterness and vindictiveness. Today's teachers of hatred, both here and abroad, are the perpetrators of tomorrow's violence. Let us be careful lest we commend to our children prejudices that grow into hatred based upon differences in religion, geography, skin color, and politics. I pray that none of our children ever will cheer someone else's hurt. This week's hate crime on a global scale calls attention to the evil of hate crimes on any scale.

Rachel is weeping for her children and refuses to be consoled.

I weep before thoughts of a loss of freedom. So many times this past week I have recalled Robert Frost's insightful words about fear. The national poet laureate once observed that he feared nothing more than people who are afraid, explaining that people who are afraid will give up even essential liberties for a modicum of security.

So, what of our tears today? Are they only tears of pain? Do they contain any hint of promise? Please know that not even the inconsolable tears of Rachel were completely devoid of promise. The same is true of our tears.

This ancient poetry of pathos contains a comforting secret. God takes our hurt into the divine nature and God hurts with us. Some interpreters of today's text believe that the voice heard weeping in Ramah was none other than the voice of the heart of God. Rachel was a God-figure. God would not be consoled over the loss of the children of God.

Now here is the public truth within that secret consolation. God is. Despite a reign of terror, despite the tragic and massive loss of life, despite our fears and sorrows, God is. God is with us! And that reality changes everything else.

In the original setting of the text about Rachel, there came the realization that the exiles eventually would return home—hear the declaration of Jeremiah, "says the Lord, they shall come back"—because God is. Note the setting of the passage in the Gospel according to Matthew. Ponder the significance of the verse that follows the poetry about Rachel. "But when Herod died, behold, an angel of the Lord appeared in a dream to Joseph" (Matt. 2:18). Look! Look at the juxtaposition of two truths—the king died and God inspired a dream. Kings come and go, tyrants die, terrorists are consumed in terror, but God remains. God is. And the God who is, this God who weeps inconsolably over the loss of God's children, inspires dreams of another day, a better day, a time of healing and deliverance, a time of comfort and peace.

So our tears of pain are also tears of promise. Amid hurt we can find hope. The terror of today is not forever. The certainty of God is a truth even surer than the verity of pain. The end can only be described by glory.

Oh, to be sure, the pain is not diminished by the promise. Those who are weeping should not stop until their tears have fully expressed their grief. But our tears, like our laughter, lead inexorably to the God who is. And the God who is ultimately comforts us, equips us to meet the challenges of our darkest hour, and leads us to the lofty places that are our true home.

The Worst Things and the Last Things

﷽

John R. Claypool

The Reverend Dr. John Claypool, from Trinity Episcopal Church in New Orleans and McAfee School of Theology in Mercer University in Atlanta, preached at First Presbyterian Church in Atlanta on September 16, 2001. He closes his sermon with these thoughts.

THERE IS A MYSTERIOUS OTHER in these places of extremity Who, like the alchemists of old, is somehow able to take one thing and transmute it into something else. We encounter this image of hopefulness in Holy Scripture and there is no better example of it than the story in Genesis that comes to its climax in our Old Testament reading this morning.

The central figure here was a man named Joseph, who was born into a tragically dysfunctional family. His father, Jacob, had truly loved only one woman in all his life—the cherished Rachel; but, for some reason, she could not bear children, which, in that day, was considered a terrible blight. According to the custom of that time, other wives were brought in to produce children, and they bore Jacob ten sons. Then, mysteriously, Rachel did conceive a child and gave birth to Joseph. This meant that Joseph was the eleventh of Jacob's children, but the firstborn of beloved Rachel.

When Rachel died giving birth to a second son, Jacob channeled all of his affection upon little Joseph and treated him differently from all the others. This created an explosive family mix, to say the least. The older brothers despised their father and his prized little pet, Joseph, who became exceedingly spoiled by all this favoritism. Everything was given to him and nothing was asked of him. Jacob even gave him a garment that was most unusual in that day, a coat with sleeves, reserved for those who did not have to do physical work.

One day, when his father insensitively sent Joseph out to check on his brothers who were working in the fields, their frustration exploded and they almost killed him with their bare hands. However, wiser heads prevailed and they settled for selling him to some Midianite slave traders headed for Egypt. They dipped in blood that famous "coat of many colors," and told their father that his precious son must have been killed by a wild beast.

Everything about this saga was soaked with genuine evil—but wait, this seemingly worst thing was not the last thing. God, the ingenious alchemist, was very much at work in all of this. When Joseph was sold to a man named Potiphar and, for the first time in his life, responsibilities were given him, he began to flower in ways he might never have developed had he stayed with his doting old father. He rose to the top quickly in Potiphar's household staff, only to have Lady Potiphar set out to seduce him sexually. When he responded repeatedly that he was not eligible for that kind of relationship, she turned the tables on him in fury and accused him of doing the very thing that she was doing instead. As a result, Joseph was cast into the depths of the royal prison.

Once again, it seemed that the very worst thing had happened to Joseph, but this alchemist God was still at work seeing to it that it was not the last thing. In prison, Joseph became known as a skillful interpreter of dreams; and when the Pharaoh began to be troubled by disturbing images in the night, someone remembered the young Hebrew prisoner's gift and Joseph was brought to the Pharaoh's attention. Joseph discerned that the great prosperity that Egypt was enjoying then would need to be carefully husbanded because a period of famine lay ahead. The Pharaoh was so impressed with Joseph's ability that he elevated him to the number two position of power in all of Egypt and placed him in charge of conserving their prosperity. Thus, when the famine did strike, Egypt became regarded as the breadbasket of the world, which caused Joseph's family in Palestine to come there to seek food.

Ultimately, because of Joseph's wisdom, the descendants of Abraham were saved from extinction. Joseph moved his whole family to Egypt, and when Jacob died, his brothers feared that Joseph might seek revenge upon them for what they had done to him so long ago. At this point comes the most dramatic statement of our text. After reflecting over the years, Joseph said to his brothers, "Be not afraid, You meant what you did for evil, but God used it for good."

Here is the essence of the hope at the heart of the Christian vision: God has the incredible ingenuity to take bad things and mysteriously bring good out of them. I ask you, is there any reality more needed just now than access to this kind of hope? September 11 of this year will go down in history as a true watershed in our national saga. It was an event that will be used to define before and after for decades to come. I need not belabor the point that we are in an unprecedented era of peril and our two great temptations will be either to give up in despair or to blow up in rage, only to make a bad situation worse.

What we need most of all is an awareness of our partnership with this alchemist God of Holy Scripture. This One did not cause those acts of terrorism by any stretch of the imagination for, in order for us to know God's kind of joy and not be robots, we had to be given the gift of freedom. What those depraved terrorists did on that fateful Tuesday was a tragic abuse of what God intended. However, the Holy One is very much involved in all of this and has the power to bring hope and healing out of this chaos. The possibilities are very real of our seeing more clearly into the true nature of evil and resolving to do differently with our lives. We are already witnessing a remarkable humanizing of life all over the world. We can become more compassionate and Christlike in the wake of this tragedy; and the basis of such a hope is our trust in the One for Whom the worst things are never the last things.

Madeleine L'Engle has just written a beautiful little novel based on a quote from a fourteenth-century mystic that states, "All the evil that human beings have ever conceived or done is no more to the mercy of God than a live coal is to the sea." This image reflects profoundly the true proportions of reality. It is reminiscent of St. Paul's words, "Where sin abounds, Grace abounds even more." God's goodness is finally bigger than all our badness, and God's power to redeem is greater than our power to sin. There is only one God. Nothing else is as big. I invite you to embrace such a vision this morning and leave this place in a spirit of hopefulness rather than despair.

Winston Churchill obviously held these beliefs. In June of 1965 he was asked to give a commencement address at a university in Great Britain. By this time, the great statesman was badly infirmed. In fact, he was within months of his own death. He had to be helped to the podium that day, and stood there saying nothing for what seemed like an interminable period. But then, that amazing voice that had once called Britain back from the brink sounded for the last time in public, and what he said was, "Never, never give up! Never give up!" Then he turned and went back to his seat. There was a moment of stunned silence, and then everyone rose to their feet in admiring applause. They say it is the only commencement address in history to be remembered verbatim by everyone who heard it. What was so powerful about it was that the words were so congruent with the one who said them. Again and again, Churchill's career had been pronounced dead, but he kept coming back. Why? Because he, too, had caught the gleam from the pages of Holy Scripture that the worst things are never the last things.

The account of Churchill's funeral at St. Paul's Cathedral confirms this fact. He had carefully planned it himself and included in it some of the great hymns of the church and all of the wonder of our Anglican liturgy. Furthermore, there were two things that he specifically requested at the end that made it unforgettable for every person there. When the benediction had been said from the high altar, silence fell over the packed cathedral. A bugler high up in the dome of St. Paul's had been asked to play the familiar sound of "Taps," a well-known signal marking the end of something. Those haunting notes brought home to everyone there the realization that an era had come to an end, and it was reported that there was hardly a dry eye in the church. However, as Churchill had requested, after the notes of "Taps" had sounded, another bugler on the other side of the dome began to play "Reveille": "It's time to get up, it's time to get up, it's time to get up in the morning." That final touch caught everyone by surprise but revealed where Churchill had gotten the strength across the years to never give up. He did believe that the worst things are never the last things and the final sounds of history will not be "Taps" but "Reveille."

How Can Everything Be All Right?

Alvin O'Neal Jackson

*The Reverend Dr. Alvin O'Neal Jackson is senior pastor of
the National City Church of Christ in Washington, D.C.,
and has served on the national board and administrative
committee of the Christian Church (Disciples of Christ).*

IN THE STILLNESS AND QUIET OF THIS MOMENT, I
want to offer a gift. Listen, if you are trying hard to
believe in God while a hundred voices on the inside are
telling you to stop believing, then this gift is for you. If
you have prayed long and hard, but your problems,
your pressures, your pain, your perplexities remain,
nothing has changed, then this gift is for you. You see
the evil, the suffering of the innocent, the injustice in
our world, and you sometimes wonder, Does God
care? And you ask, How can everything be all right
when everything is all wrong? This gift is for you!

I sat the other day with family members who had
lost loved ones in the Pentagon bombing. Several
members of our congregation lost family members

there. As I was leaving the room where family members had gathered for a briefing by members of the Pentagon staff on the recovery of their loved ones, a father who had lost a son came up to me and whispered, "Pastor, it's all right." Yes, I said, it's all right. But I must confess that deep in my heart I wondered how could it be all right when everything appeared all wrong. It was all wrong for this young man's wife. It was all wrong for his children. It was all wrong for his friends. It was all wrong for his parents. And I found myself asking as I rode down the elevator to the parking garage, How can it be all right when everything is all wrong?

How can it be all right? We say it all the time: "It's all right." A boy strikes out in a little league game and his coach says, "Son, it's all right. A guest spills coffee on a clean tablecloth and the hostess says, "It's all right." But deeper than that — not just a crying baby or spilled milk or a missed ball, but life at its depths — when you are staring death in the face, how can it be all right, when your whole world is falling apart . . . how can it be all right? Is it just a cliché to say it's all right? Is it profound self-deception or uncommon truth? How can it be all right when everything is all wrong? I have been wrestling with that. I have been struggling with that question and Paul helped me out. The Apostle Paul had a saying. It was a little commonplace pleasantry, a cliché, a trivial custom, a simple platitude. For most people it didn't mean much of anything, just something you said in polite conversation. If you had been living in Paul's day, you would have heard it everywhere Greek was spoken. A man lifts a glass of wine to a stranger he meets in a bar and he might say, "Here's grace to you." Or you might sign off on a letter to a person you despise and you might say, "Grace be with you." It was just a stale, flip, silly little line people used to oil the machinery of trivial conversation. It was just a commonplace saying, nothing more. It was like saying, "Good luck to you," "Be cool," "It's all right." Doesn't mean much of anything, just something to say.

But Paul took this little anemic commonplace saying and rescued it and gave it a whole new meaning. Nearly every letter he wrote, he opened with, "Grace be with you," and he closed with, "Grace be with you." And here in this fifth chapter of Romans Paul puts a theological spotlight on this word "grace" and dips it into a whole new reality. And grace becomes the signal of God's assurance that life can be all right when everything is all wrong. Grace becomes a kind of shorthand for everything God is and for everything God does in our lives. And so when you want to talk about God, about who he is and about what he has done for us, all you have to do is say grace. Grace makes it all right even though everything is all wrong. And so I come this morning to offer the gift of grace. Grace, God's grace, not a cliché, not just a word without meaning, not just another theological doctrine, but the very gift of God. Not an abstract theoretical idea, not a trick or a ticket to some fantasy island, not some esoteric, ethereal notion, not some pie in the sky in the sweet bye and bye, but grace is that which allows us to look at earthly reality with all of its problems and pain, with all its hurts and heartbreaks, with all its sad and tragic edges and cruel cuts, and still be able to say at the very center of our being, "It's all right." That's why we call it amazing grace!

I come this morning to offer the gift of God's amazing grace. And this gift of grace has at least three handles, and if you can grab all three, you are on your way to real life. The first handle of grace is pardon. The bedrock of grace is the amazing gift of knowing that it is all right with us personally when we know that a lot of things are wrong with us. God knows that our life is not all together. God knows that we keep messing up. God knows we keep turning our back on him, He knows our inner struggle. He sees the selfish motivation, even when we do something good. He sees the gap between our ought-ness and our is-ness. He sees that we are all vogue on the outside, but all vague on the inside. But he looks at us in all of our wretchedness and says, "I pardon you. I love you. I accept you. I forgive you. I receive you." We have been pardoned. Grace says we are pardoned.

The second handle of grace is power, power to lead us closer to God's image and make us better people today than we were yesterday. But we will not sense how amazing this power is unless we see that it is unlike any energy we manipulate through our technology. Grace is a power totally unlike any we created in nuclear reactors; it is different from all physical force. But it is different, too, from moral force; grace does not make us better people by bullying us into moral improvement. The power to make us better works when God freely persuades us that it is all right with us the way we are. The power of grace is paradoxical. For the moment when we know it's all right, even though we are grotesquely in the wrong, we are liberated from our private burden of failures and given power to become the sort of person God wants us to be.

But not only is grace power and pardon. The third handle of grace is promise. The power of promise to live now as if things are going to be all right tomorrow. Things might not be all right now, but grace is promise. Paul said, "We boast in our sufferings, knowing that suffering produces endurance, and endurance character and character produces hope, and hope does not disappoint us."

They can slay the dreamer, but never kill the dream. They can murder the prophet, but never stop the proclamation. They can excoriate the preacher, but never exterminate the Gospel. They can stone people, but never stop God. Right will win. Truth crushed to earth will rise again. God will rule. Every knee will bow. Every tongue will confess. The wicked will cease from troubling, and the weary will be at rest. Weeping endures for a night, but joy comes in the morning. Grace always has the last word.

Monday and Tuesday, September 17–18

Rosh HaShanah Services

Rosh HaShanah Evening Homily

Peter Rubinstein

On the evening of Rosh HaShanah, inaugurating the Jewish Days of Awe, the congregation of Central Synagogue gathered in their home for the first time in three years, following a fire that had destroyed their sanctuary. Senior Rabbi Peter Rubinstein and the other rabbis who serve this New York congregation each delivered this homily at services held throughout the synagogue.

THESE ARE SOMBER DAYS. Though gathering for typically a joyful occasion of the new year, we enter this year, 5762, with a sadness and vicious weight bearing heavily upon us. The comforting cloak of innocence has been rudely stripped from our shoulders. Never again will we contend that the violence of terror is cordoned off far away from our shores.

Enemies have come to our nation, to our city. They trapped us in our homes and offices and airplanes. They perforated what we thought was an impenetrable armor of security. And they established a new benchmark for evil. The Holocaust remains the severest measure of genocide. This heartrending episode expands horror and terror to a previously inconceivable measure. These high holidays are without compare.

We are reeling. We suffer powerful, uncontrollable emotions. We are afraid and sad. We are angry and anguished. We are bewildered and battered. More than before we know that destiny is beyond our control.

This we know also . . . that in more than one way, the World Trade Center was a symbol of the best of America. Lost in its rubble were Americans of sixty national backgrounds, from a vast array of ethnic and religious convictions, from the spectrum of economic and social class. It didn't matter who we were. The terrorists struck every one of us. No one can say the tragedy is someone else's challenge. Together we are one. We weep together and we cling together. Together as one, we are thankful to the New York City Police and Fire Departments and emergency services and personnel and hospitals and doctors and nurses and the volunteers from around this country and world who are working tirelessly, themselves suffering tremendous loss. Some of them are here this evening. Together as one, we mourn with them.

Together as one we will pursue justice. We are determined to hunt down and destroy the machinery of evil. It will require patience. It will require trust. It may require trial and error. It will require perseverance over years.

Together as one, we will talk of pain and agony. We

will cry and hold each other, sometimes with words, sometimes in whispers, and sometimes in silence. We are not poets or elegists. We do not know how to speak of such horror. So we tell stories, and we must, of those who are lost, those for whom we still have hope and those for whom hope has given way to the sad reality of death. We sing their songs. We raise our voices to the vaults of heaven to call to them, to tell them of our love, to pray that God care for them, and to continue the melodies of their lives. We will proclaim the ground where they died as sacred ground. Like wisps of billowing smoke, their souls hover above us.

Together as one, we are anguished and frightened. We yearn for protection from God, from our government, from a carefully woven safety net. Yet, we now understand vulnerability to a degree beyond any conceived before.

Of God we will ask, "How can this happen? Should not evil be vanquished and the good and just be raised on high?" Of our authorities we wonder, What did we miss?

It may not yet be time for questions. We barely hang on, each minute feeling like an hour, the past week feeling like forever. We are glued to the television, needing to see and at the same time being repulsed by the images of horror and affliction.

We are reminded in the book of Ecclesiastes (3:1–4):

> *To everything there is a season*
> *and a time to every purpose under the heavens.*

a time to be born and a time to die,
a time to plant and a time to uproot that
which is planted,
a time for weeping and a time
for laughing,
a time for wailing and a time
for dancing.

In the most somber and saddest of days, together as one, we wonder how will there be again a time for laughter and joy and dance? How could we find within the capacity to burst forth again with joyous singing? How can we feel the heartaches of our own losses or look into the tear-stained eyes of those who are missing family members and friends, fiancés and lovers, and talk about hope and renewal?

It is difficult to know when we will turn the corner and feel committed again to better days. It is difficult to know when we will believe that there will be a time to sing and dance, when the pall under which we function like the smoke that hangs above the World Trade Center will be carried away by time.

But this we do know . . . that if you love, you grieve. There are no exceptions. Even for the stranger, we grieve.

Together as one, we will take each other's hands, hug and hold each other, and urge and help each other to move ourselves forward. This great congregation rebuilt its sanctuary. Our governor and mayor used us as a symbol in conversation with President Bush when he visited on Friday. They told the president, "Just as this congregation rebuilt, so we will rebuild!"

Our city will rebuild buildings, but we cannot replace lost life. Yet we are a people with a long and holy tradition of walking through the valley of the shadow of death, then rising to the mountains warmed by the sun to set our eyes upon the horizon. We are a people that embraces each new year with the ultimate belief that goodness will triumph over evil, that justice will "well up as waters, And righteousness as a mighty stream." We have founded ourselves upon the pillars of mercy and goodness and lifted ourselves in striving to be holy like God.

We have embraced the faith of Nehemiah who looked upon a destroyed city and proclaimed, "You see the bad state we are in—our city lying in ruins. . . . And they said, NAKUM OO-VANINYU (Let us rise up and rebuild). So they strengthened their hands for this good work" (Neh. 2:17–18).

We will rise up. We will rebuild our lives, our visions, our dreams. We will carry with us forever the names and faces and stories of those who have been taken from the face of this earth. We take them into our hearts and give them a place beside the cherished memories of our own loved ones. They now are ours.

And we will hope for and move toward better days, a gentler tomorrow. God has granted us an inexhaustible, an indomitable spirit. God has given us this creation with its abundance and beauty, forests dancing with life, mountains rising like prayers, seas roaring their creative hymn. Together we raise our hands, our hearts, our souls, and reach toward the heights, resilient, determined, strong, courageous, and compassionate.

Thus as Jews we pray, through the depth of the night. We pray to demonstrate the undying commitment of Jewish life, of life itself. We pray to affirm our trust in the ultimate decency of humanity. We pray as an act of courage and thanksgiving and gratitude to those who bravely fight to save life. We pray and remember as we mourn those who have died, and we seek healing for those who are hurt and safety for those who are still missing.

We will pray this evening for comfort and strength and hope. Thus we hold forever high the banners of conscience and decency and life. May God be with us, together as one as we lift our eyes to the mountains.

We Are All Israelis Now

Harold S. Kushner

Harold S. Kushner is rabbi laureate of Temple Israel in Natick, Massachusetts, where he delivered this message on the first morning of Rosh HaShanah. His many books include When Bad Things Happen to Good People *and* Living a Life that Matters.

I REMEMBER WHEN I WAS A BOY GROWING UP in Brooklyn that every year our beloved old rabbi (who was probably younger then than I am today) would begin the Rosh HaShanah service with a prayer whose opening words were: TICHLEH SHANAH UK'LALOTEHA, TAHEL SHANAH UVIRCHOTEHA. May the old year end with all of its calamities, and may the new year begin with all of its blessings.

And I remember that that prayer always made me uncomfortable. I would say to myself, "That prayer belongs back in Europe where life was hard and every year brought more trouble. But here the years are good." Yet yesterday and today, I found myself praying that all the killing, all the hatred, all the tears and bloodshed of these past twelve months vanish along with the old year, and that the coming year be free of all that.

But what is there to say? How does one make sense of a senseless tragedy? How does one come to terms with the knowledge that some people hate other people so much that they would kill themselves in order to kill thousands of strangers?

After the terrible events of last Tuesday, a number of colleagues I spoke to had all independently come up with the same insight: We are all Israelis now. Now all Americans know the feeling of vulnerability, of uncertainty, that Israelis feel when they go shopping, when they send their children off to school in the morning, when their sons and husbands leave for military reserve duty. And if we are all Israelis now, maybe we can learn something from Israel's fifty-three years of hard-won experience dealing with the threat of terrorism.

How do Israelis handle the danger? They go on living. They continue to shop, they continue to ride the buses, they continue to send their children to school. There is always an element of concern, which is why they compulsively listen to the news every hour on the hour. But they understand that if they ever stopped going on with their normal lives, they would be conceding, and they are not prepared to do that.

You know the story we read from the Torah on Rosh HaShanah, the story of how God commands Abraham to offer up his son as a sacrifice and then intervenes to save the boy at the last moment. In the Torah, though we don't read this far on Rosh HaShanah, the very next thing that happens is that we read of the death of Sarah, Abraham's wife and Isaac's mother. Though the Torah never makes the timeframe explicit (it could have happened years later and probably did), Jewish commentators have always suspected a link between the two events. They imagine Sarah dying immediately after and as a result of Isaac's near-death experience. One midrash has Satan telling Sarah that Isaac has been killed, and Sarah dying of grief. Another pictures Satan telling Sarah what really happened, that Isaac was almost killed but was spared, and Sarah dies anyway. Why? The midrash doesn't try to explain it, but Aviva Zornberg, a brilliant Israeli Bible scholar, understands it in this way: Sarah dies of despair because she can't stand living in a world that random and unreliable, a world where life hangs by a thread every day. How can you live in a world where you say good-bye to your loved ones in the morning and you can't be certain you will ever see each other again? All that uncertainty is too much for her.

This week I suspect a lot of people are feeling like Sarah did. They are saying to themselves, "How do you live in a world like this?" They are asking, "Where can I move to, how can I change my way of living so that I don't have to be in danger?"

To those questions, Israelis, I think, have given us the answer. For the most part, they have rejected

Sarah's reaction to the threat of terror. They have squared their shoulders, summoned up their courage, and gone on with their lives. And I would hope that all Americans, now that we know the vulnerability that Israelis have been living with, will do the same.

I intend to get back on airplanes when airports re-open and my schedule calls for me to fly somewhere. I was on a plane at Logan last Tuesday, planning to travel to Toronto, when we got word that all flights had been canceled everywhere, and I will be back flying again after the holidays. I will not let the terrorists tell me how I can live. I will not let them keep me from doing the things I want to do, not my business travel and not my traveling to visit family. I will act prudently and carefully, but I will refuse to let them control my life or shrink the boundaries of what I feel safe doing.

I understand the Torah's admonition "Choose Life" to mean, "Don't be afraid of living." Don't be afraid to live, even though living may be painful or precarious. Do you want to get even with the people who did that to us last week? You know how to do that? I would paraphrase F. Scott Fitzgerald who said, "Living well is the best revenge." My adage would read, "Living normally, living bravely is the best revenge."

A second concern is how we as a nation will respond to what was done to us. Ever since Tuesday, we have felt hurt and angry and most significantly we have felt helpless. There seemed to be so little we could do to help the victims or to hurt the perpetrators. And when a person feels helpless, there is an almost irresistible impulse to do something to reclaim power, to restore a feeling of being in charge. That's why the most sobering comment I heard all week was from a caller to a radio station who quoted the adage "Be careful whom you see as an enemy for you will become like them." Last week the danger to America was from stolen airplanes and falling buildings. Today the danger to America is that, out of our pain and rage, we will forget what we stand for as a people. We will betray precisely those values that our enemies hate us for. The perpetrators of last week's atrocities earned our contempt by killing innocent people in what they believed was a just cause. It's important that we never become contemptible ourselves by becoming like them, by scapegoating innocent Muslims or American Arabs who share our values not theirs, by raining bombs or missiles on somebody, anybody, just to feel powerful again. I would hope that we will identify and punish the people and the governments behind last week's event, and punish them thoroughly. I'm old enough to remember how we did that after Pearl Harbor. A movie about Pearl Harbor puts these words in the mouth of the Japanese admiral: "I fear we awakened a sleeping giant and filled him with a terrible resolve." And I expect that the same thing will happen again. But I hope that America never stops being America in the process of bringing people to justice.

We learned another lesson on Tuesday, one that maybe we should have known before but we needed last week's terrible tragedy to make clear to us. After we heard of the horrific events in New York and Washington, we canceled religious school classes and sent your children home. We weren't entirely sure why we were doing it. The prospect of a terrorist attack on the temple was fairly remote. After terrorists had struck the World Trade Center and the Pentagon, nobody really believed that Temple Israel of Natick was next on their list. But somehow it seemed like the right thing to do. And when we called you to tell you what we were doing, you thanked us for it.

Only later did I understand why. At a time like that, we want our family around us. We want to know that they are safe, and we want them to know that we are safe. At a time like that, we don't want to be alone. We want to be able to hug somebody, to talk to somebody, even just to watch the news on television with somebody rather than be alone. We learned something about why we need our families.

And then on Wednesday and Thursday, the stories began to come out about some of the people who died in the plane crashes or in the office buildings, and now there were faces and stories to go with the names and numbers. And just as hearing the number Six Million does not help many of us to comprehend the Holocaust, reading *The Diary of Anne Frank* helps us begin to understand. We began to understand just what was lost last week when we heard personal stories. Many of the people were from the Boston area. Some of them were prominent businessmen, founders of high-tech firms, executives of major corporations. But nobody talked about that. People spoke only of what loving husbands and wives, what special fathers and mothers they were, how much they gave to the community. And if we are desperate to find something good and redemptive in this shattering tragedy, that might be it: that is what all of us will be remembered for. Not our accomplishments, not our successes, but the love we shared with the people around us.

This, after all, is the season for confronting our mortality, for facing up to the unsettling truth that none of us knows how long we have to live. B'ROSH HASHANAH YIKATEVUN UV'YOM TZOM KIPPUR YEHATEMUN, It is decreed on Rosh HaShanah and confirmed on Yom Kippur, MI YICHYEH UMI YAMUT, who shall live and who shall die, who by sword and who by fire. I don't think the prayer asks us to believe that God decided last September that these thousands of people would not live to see another autumn and that the terrorists were doing God's will. I think the prayer comes to warn us that, because life is precarious, make sure you start doing the things that really matter, the things that will ultimately win you your immortality.

How do we make our lives matter to the world? The answer is, we do it by loving the people around us. If you have known the feeling of loving someone and being loved by someone, you have changed someone's life and by so doing, you changed the world.

There is another prayer we recite on Rosh HaShanah. We say it several times in the course of the first and second Amidah prayers. We say it individually and then we go back and say it with the congregation. It begins: UV'CHAN TZADDIKIM YIR'U V'YISMACHU VIY'SHARIM YA'ALOZU . . . V'CHOL HARISHA KULA KE'ASHAN TICHLEH. May this coming year be a year in which good people will have reason to rejoice, a year in which wickedness will be silenced and evil vanish like smoke, for God will remove the dominion of arrogance from the world.

And that, perhaps more than any other single line from the Mahzor, is our prayer today: May this year give good people reason to rejoice for what happens in the world, when we see God's world cleansed of hatred and wickedness.

The Ongoing Challenge

A Challenge to Christians

Frank T. Griswold

The Most Reverend Frank T. Griswold, presiding bishop and primate of the Episcopal Church, United States of America, preached this sermon at the House of Bishops' Meeting in St. Paul's Cathedral, Burlington, Vermont, on Sunday, September 23.

WHEN WE FIND OURSELVES PERSONALLY and corporately in "thin places," as Evelyn Underhill calls them, it is often the words of scripture, charged as they are with the joys and sorrows, the burdens and yearnings of our forebears in faith that give voice to that which is deep within us and name emotions of which we may hardly be aware.

By virtue of the events of September 11, we now in the United States join that company of nations in which ideology disguised as true religion wreaks havoc and sudden death. The invincible is shown to be vulnerable and in that moment the door is opened which, if we choose to pass through it, will lead us beyond death and destruction into a new solidarity with those for whom the evil forces of terrorism are a continuing fear and reality.

Lamentation, however, is not an end in itself, but rather it opens the way to the question, "Why?" which leads in turn to self-scrutiny and self-examination. What might we learn from what we have suffered and are suffering — about ourselves, and about ourselves in relationship to others? How has our consciousness been altered by what has come down so suddenly and violently upon us? What invitation emerges from that terrible fire-filled day to engage us not simply as Americans but as persons of faith?

In the Gospel reading we have just heard, Jesus declares that no slave can serve two masters and therefore we cannot serve God and wealth (Luke 16:13). What Jesus is pointing to when he speaks about service is what we might call the ground of our personal allegiance, the desire of our heart at its most radical depth: the fundamental orientation of our life.

If our life is ordered to God, we find ourselves caught up in God's mercy and compassion. God's "fierce bonding love," a mercy and compassion and love that stretches and expands us, cracks open our hearts of stone and transforms them into hearts of flesh — hearts capable of embracing others in the strength of God's all-embracing compassion.

Many centuries ago, St. Isaac of Syria, one of the great wisdom figures of the Eastern Church, raised the question: What is a merciful and compassionate heart?

He answered the question in this way:

> It is a heart which burns with love for the whole
> of creation: for humankind, for the birds, for the
> beasts, for the demons, for every creature. When
> persons with a heart such as this think of the crea-
> tures or look at them, their eyes are filled with tears.
> An overwhelming compassion makes their heart
> grow small and weak, and they cannot endure to
> hear or see any suffering, even the smallest pain, in-
> flicted upon any creature. Therefore, they never
> cease to pray with tears even for the irrational ani-
> mals, for the enemies of truth and for those who do
> them evil asking that those for whom they pray may
> be guarded and receive God's mercy. And for the
> reptiles also they pray with a great compassion,
> which rises endlessly in their hearts until they shine
> again and are glorious like God.

This all-embracing compassion, which can include
beasts and demons, enemies and reptiles, is beyond our
effort and imagination. It is a gift. It is the consequence
of Christ being formed in us, our being conformed to
Christ, which is what our baptism into Christ and our
weekly sharing of the eucharist is all about.

To serve God, therefore, is not a frantic execution
of self-chosen tasks that we hope will please the
Almighty, but about the mind and heart of Christ
being worked in us by the Spirit so that our compassion, our just-ness are revelatory of the One who, from
the cross, draws the world, all people and all things, to
himself, in his loving embrace.

A life ordered to wealth yields a very different fruit. Whereas compassion turns us outward in relationship to the world around us, wealth on its own disconnects us and turns us in on ourselves in self-serving defensiveness. And here wealth is not simply money but includes such things as status, ethnicity, color, education, culture, nationality, religion, and more.

Wealth is both personal and corporate. We speak, for example, of our nation's wealth, and from it follows what we call "our national interests," which are to be defended at all costs.

In the light of the traumatic events of these past days, which have claimed and touched so many lives — the lives not only of our own citizens but those of other nations as well — are we not in a spirit of lamentation invited to ask questions about ourselves and, as a nation, engage in the solemn task of self-examination?

Unquestionably, the attack on September 11 was an evil and deranged act fueled by a zeal in which God the Compassionate One is transmuted into a God of suicide, murder, and destruction. That being clearly said, is there not, as we seek to build a coalition of nations to join us in a war on terrorism, an invitation to examine our national interests in relationship to the global community of which we are a part?

In what ways do our own interests and their uncritical pursuit affect other nations and the welfare of their people? How are we as a nation "under God," as we call ourselves, being invited to reorder our life according to God's compassion for "humankind and for every creature"?

We, who so easily quit the global table when the conditions are not to our liking or do not serve our economic interests, are called to yield our wealth in service to God's all-embracing compassion, which is the heart of God's just-ness and God's desire for the world. Just as our efforts to disarm terrorism will require discipline and sacrifice, so too will the reordering of our national interests to serve the global family of which we are now a part in a new and vulnerable way.

The way of compassion transfigures and heals not simply those to whom it is directed, but those who practice it. Those who allow God's compassion to well up in their hearts "shine and are glorious like God," or as Isaiah says of those who inhabit compassion: "Your light shall break forth like the dawn; and your healing shall spring up quickly" (Isa. 58:8).

God's project, and therefore the Church's mission, is one of reconciliation: "to restore all people to unity with God and each other in Christ" (2 Cor. 5:18). And God's compassion, God's mercy, God's loving kindness, God's fierce bonding love is the active principle that effects reconciliation: the gathering up of all things into a unity in which difference is both honored and reconciled in the fullness of God's ever-creative imagination.

May each of us who have been baptized into Christ be given a compassionate heart in the service of reconciliation, and may we as a nation seek our healing not through revenge and retaliation, but by "sharing our bread with the hungry" across the world. Only in that way can our light truly break forth like the dawn and our healing spring up quickly.

A Challenge to People
of All Faiths

Harvey Cox

*Harvey Cox, professor of divinity at Harvard, delivered these
remarks at an interfaith breakfast on September 25 in
Boston at the Church of the New Jerusalem. He is the
author of many books, including, most recently,* Common
Prayers: Faith, Family and a Christian's Journey
Through the Jewish Year.

> *By the waters of Babylon we sat down and wept*
> *As we remembered Zion.*
> *On the willow trees there*
> *We hung up our lyres,*
> *For those who had carried us captive*
> *Asked us to sing a song,*
> *Our captors called on us to be joyful:*
> *"Sing us one of the songs of Zion,"*
> *How could we sing the Lord's song*
> *In a strange land?* (Psalm 137:1-4)

WE WOKE UP IN AMERICA on September 11,
2001, in a familiar setting. But by the end of the
day, we all felt we were living in a strange land. Except

for the pile of smoking debris where the Twin Towers had stood, the landscape was the same. But otherwise our country seemed strange and alien. We were still at home, but it was no longer the home we were accustomed to, a comfortable island with oceans around us, immune to the fear and foreboding that roam so much of the earth. We had become part of humanity in a new and painful way. Hearing this Psalm, and realizing that others—in history and in other lands—have also experienced this kind of suffering and this uncanny feeling, was somehow comforting.

But this Psalm also carried another message, one that we are more reluctant to hear. Its final verses read as follows:

> *Babylon, Babylon the destroyer*
> *Happy is he who repays you*
> *For what you did to us!*
> *Happy is he who seizes your babes*
> *And dashes them against a rock.* (Psalm 137: 8–9)

A beautiful paean ends with an ugly cry for revenge and slaughter. No wonder the psalm is hardly ever read in its entirety.

Much has been said in the past few days about how religion can incite, or at least condone, violence. But when you listen, it is usually the other person's religion, not mine, that does the condoning. The harsh truth, however, is that virtually every religious tradition has spawned violent episodes during its history and enshrines "texts of terror" in its scriptures. The Jewish and Christian traditions are no exception. Psalm 137 is only one example among many in our own Bible. The West Bank settlers point to passages from the book of Joshua which they maintain command them to "conquer and settle" regardless of the rights of the Palestinians who live there. Fundamentalist Christians seize upon the flamboyant book of Revelation to sanction apocalyptic savagery. Hindus are now using their scriptures to authorize the destruction of mosques.

For centuries adherents of a religion have often soft-pedaled their own ugly texts and violent histories and have emphasized their most positive features. Christians talked about St. Francis and tried to ignore Torquemada. Jews quoted Rabbi Abraham Joshua Heschel and not Rabbi Meyer Kahane. But now the situation is both more urgent and more complex. As religious diversity widens and interfaith dialogue spreads, people of faith have an understandable desire to emphasize the peaceful elements not only in our own traditions, but in others as well. We want to present all religions in their best light. The result is often a certain lack of frankness. We do not ask the hard questions, either of others or of ourselves. But simply making nice does not contribute to genuine dialogue. We now need to take another step in interfaith dialogue, to move from courtliness to candor. We must acknowledge that we all have "texts of terror." We wish they were not there, but they are. They lie there like dry tinder, and any spark could set them ablaze. Coping with their meaning in today's world is a pressing task we need to tackle together.

We gain nothing by claiming that those who foment violence in God's name are not "real" Jews or Christians or "real" Hindus or Muslims. They insist they are, and say that we who disagree with their rancorous views are the impostors. We try to read them out; they try to read us out. But that argument leads nowhere. A more promising way to proceed is to ask why and when texts, which are most often read to apply to spiritual struggle, sometimes burst into the flames of actual carnage. This is not an easy problem.

Gandhi, a Hindu, was the world's most exemplary practitioner of nonviolence. Yet his favorite text was the Bhagavad Gita. In it the warrior prince Arguna, on the day before leading his troops into battle, finds it horrifying to contemplate the bloodshed the fighting will exact. He perspires and trembles so uncontrollably that his sword nearly falls from his hand. He feels he cannot go through with it. But the god Krishna commands him to go ahead and fight because it is his caste duty. Gandhi was a courageous foe of both caste and warfare. Yet this story was his inspiration. How could that be? Because he read it as a call to all human beings to struggle against violence and hatred, to accept wounds rather than inflict them, and to overcome enmity with what he called "soul force."

Scriptures do not have fixed meanings, as the patchwork history of their many interpretations clearly demonstrates. They mean different things to different people at different times. Nor are scriptures monolithic. What draws some Christians to the Sermon on the Mount and others to sanguinary scenes of Final Judgment? Why do some Jews cherish Isaiah's words about beating swords into plowshares, while others quote the command to slay all the Amalakites? Our common task as people of faith today is an urgent one. It is to locate those circumstances, often created by poverty, resentment, ignorance, and isolation, when texts of spiritual struggle fuel actual violence, to understand the factors that tempt people into using their scriptures to justify hatred and brutality. All traditions share the problem. And the venom erupts both within them and among them. So we must call each other to account and help each other. We cannot do this alone. The era of genteel interfaith circumlocution is over. What we need now is frank interfaith soul-searching.

Benediction

≽≼

John M. Buchanan

*The Reverend Dr. John M. Buchanan is senior minister of
Fourth Presbyterian Church in Chicago, Illinois, and editor
of the* Christian Century *magazine. He closed his sermon
of September 23 with these words.*

FRIDAY AFTERNOON I had been invited to speak at a
memorial service at Holy Name Cathedral for the
United Airlines flight crews that were lost on September 11 on Flight 175 and Flight 93.

The service was sponsored by the Flight Attendants
Organization and the Association of Airline Pilots.
Holy Name Cathedral was full of United Airlines blue
uniforms, men and women, one week and three days
after an act that had violently killed eighteen of their
friends. It was a vulnerable congregation: proud pro-
fessionals who were feeling understandably helpless
and vulnerable. They have felt the full brunt of this
thing. In the loss of friends, a terrible reminder
of the danger of their work, and now, to add more

cruelty, economic forces that seem to threaten their jobs and the entire industry.

I reached for words. I told them that they were our neighbors, our airline in Chicago that had taken us where we needed to go and brought us safely home. I told them we were grateful for them and proud of them, that God loved their friends who died and that God loved them too.

There were eighteen candles on the high altar at Holy Name. As a Pentecostal choir sang a stirring version of "The Battle Hymn of the Republic," eighteen flight attendants and pilots lined up at the altar and each lighted a candle to honor a dear, dead colleague. We sang "America the Beautiful" and "Amazing Grace." Father Bob McLaughlin led us in a prayer and sent us out into the world in peace. I was drained, tired, weary, and a little discouraged at my own inadequacy to find the words to help.

And then walking up State Street, with my pulpit robe over my arm and a clerical collar on, I was spotted by a street person singing "Take Me out to the Ball Game" at the top of his lungs. They look for clerical collars—we're easy—and I saw him coming and reached for my wallet. "Father," he said (that's what happens when you wear a clerical collar on State Street), "Father, there's one God, right?" "Well, yes, there is one God," I responded, thinking, "This is really going to be an expensive one." "So if there's only one God, then we're all sort of the same, right?" And I had to agree with that too. And then he said, "Cheer up, Father, we're all going to be okay." And he did the most extraordinary thing, he pointed upward, like an Olympic athlete or like the Cubs relief pitcher Flash Gordon, who, when he gets the final out and nails down the win, raises his arm and points an index finger straight up to the heavens. It's an act of defiant hope, after a moment of extreme vulnerability. And I joined him, pointing up to the heavens. He said it again: "We're going to be okay, Father."

We believe that God, the sovereign Lord of history, is out in front of us, summoning us.

We dare to believe that even when we face uncertainty, danger, and fear, it is an act of faithfulness and defiant hope to lift our eyes and look up to the future to which God calls us.

"We're going to be okay."

Amen.

Acknowledgments

⁂

T HIS BOOK REPRESENTS the collaborative effort of
dozens of people. Its inspiration came in a call
from my St. Martins editor, Tim Bent, who advised me
all along the way. My literary agent, Neeti Madan of
Sterling Lord Agency, elicited the interest of several
publishing houses, a major feat given that all profits
from the book would be going to charity. I am especially grateful to Helene Atwan, publisher of Beacon
Press, for her thoughtful encouragement. The enthusi-
asm and direction offered by George Gibson and Beth
Walker at Walker Publishing Company have been
both extraordinary and invaluable. Having worked
before with all three of these great houses, I feel triply
blessed to have been associated with the wonderful
people at each of them.

Three individuals made my recent life much easier by seeding the clouds for sermons. My ministerial colleagues C. Welton Gaddy, executive director of the Interfaith Alliance, and Bob Hill, minister of the Church of Christ in Kansas City, offered tireless assistance. Gustav Neibuhr, religion editor of the *New York Times*, was incredibly generous with both time (which he didn't have) and advice (which he possesses in fruitful abundance). Given how quickly I had to move, I simply could not have done this without their help.

My All Souls staff has risen to the occasion as they always do. I wish particularly to thank Megan Martin, Candice Thompson, Annie Gorycki, and Susanne May.

Finally, I wish to thank each of those who shared their sermons with me. I could easily have put together a volume many times this size without any appreciable drop in quality. Clergy are often the last people to receive pastoral care. Through the gift of these sermons, over the past two weeks, I have been the grateful recipient of so many healing thoughts that my life, despite the shadow cast by these times, has been inestimably enriched.

FORREST CHURCH

All royalties and profits from the sale of *Restoring Faith* are being contributed to charities benefiting the victims of the terrorist attacks of September 11, 2001.